Half-way Done

From Fear To Love

C.R.E. Gonzalez

WestBow
PRESS
A DIVISION OF THOMAS NELSON

WestBow Press books may be ordered through booksellers or by contacting:

WestBow Press
A Division of Thomas Nelson
1663 Liberty Drive
Bloomington, IN 47403
www.westbowpress.com
1-(866) 928-1240

Because of the dynamic nature of the Internet, any web addresses or links contained in this book may have changed since publication and may no longer be valid. The views expressed in this work are solely those of the author and do not necessarily reflect the views of the publisher, and the publisher hereby disclaims any responsibility for them.

Any people depicted in stock imagery provided by Thinkstock are models, and such images are being used for illustrative purposes only.

Certain stock imagery © Thinkstock.

This book is a work of non-fiction. Unless otherwise noted, the author and the publisher make no explicit guarantees as to the accuracy of the information contained in this book and in some cases, names of people and places have been altered to protect their privacy.

Scripture taken from the King James Version of the Bible.

ISBN: 978-1-4497-9498-9 (sc)
ISBN: 978-1-4497-9499-6 (hc)
ISBN: 978-1-4497-9497-2 (e)

Library of Congress Control Number: 2013908541

Printed in the United States of America.

WestBow Press rev. date: 5/23/2013

Introduction

When I decided to write this book, I promised myself that I would be honest even if it would mean that others would view me differently or disagree with me. I am entitled to express the voice of circumstance and the changes that have occurred in my life, and I have chosen to do so by writing.

From beginning to end, I will share with you my devastating experiences, from the time I was a child to my very difficult times as a foster mother. I will also share the joy that comes when it appears that all hope is gone. Joy surely does come in the morning.

The title of this book *Halfway Done*, came one day when I said to my husband, "I am halfway done with this book. What should I name it?" And very effortlessly he said, "Name it *Halfway Done*." I thought about it for a minute and thought it was perfect. I was about halfway done with life according to the statistical average for a person to live, and I felt halfway done with my approach to the things and people in my life. Some days I felt like a half-done meal, not thoroughly cooked. I also felt halfway done with learning how to love. I have more to learn. And from this the title was born. I hope you not only enjoy it, but find help, comfort, and truth in it. I also hope it helps you to live just a little bit lighter.

Dedication

This book is dedicated to my entire family that stretches across the country but especially my dad, mom, husband, children, six sisters, grandma Maytee, friends, and last but certainly not least, my adopted daughter, whom God allowed to emotionally dissect every part of me until I was whole. This is also dedicated to every foster parent, adoptive parent, and child everywhere who feels misunderstood and can't seem to find the stamina to continue on.

And to those of you who attempted knowingly or unknowingly to drain or destroy my spirit, I have forgiven you and remember that we all have sinned and fallen short of the glory of God. Your actions are not for me to judge but for God to judge. Judgment is better in the hands of God than in the hands of man. My prayer is that you have learned, as I have, to release your anger, unforgiveness, and heartaches to the holy one.

Blessings to you all, wherever you may be!

Table of Contents

Temporarily Insane

I had these feelings that would not go away—feelings of anger and resentment caused by not being loved properly and being sexually abused as a little girl. I was a mother struggling to find my way in my family, and let me tell you, it was not easy.

It all started years ago when I had the brilliant idea of bringing a foster child into our home. I thought I would love him or her and that the world would become a better place, all in the embrace of a hug. Boy, was I wrong! No one broke out into song, the sun did not shine brighter, the windows of heaven did not open, and our lives were not made better. As a matter of fact things got worse.

One day in May 2006, little Mary came to us as a respite child. The foster parents who were caring for her needed some relief from the stress and were trying to make the heart-wrenching decision of whether to keep her or not. In their home she had done everything, from destroying their items to urinating on things.

When I first saw her, there was no instant connection. I think I was scared out of my mind, and though I could see how cute she was with her bushy, curly hair, I knew something was not right. At that time, she was very hyperactive and had very little self-control. She had trouble focusing and seemed not to be in her right mind. Even in the midst of this, there was something tugging at me to bring her into our home. My husband agreed, though he thought I should wait, and not long afterward, she came to stay with us. I know he too wanted to help her, but at the time he said, "I am doing this because you want to do it." I think he was a little afraid too.

My husband—I love him dearly, but years ago we struggled to find a balance in our relationship because I was very emotional, and he tended to be very rigid and emotionless. However, he was really good with children, and we both had a soft spot for them—or so we thought.

After this little girl had come to us on several different occasions, the foster family she was living with could no longer deal with her behaviors, which had become too much for them to handle. At one point, she purposely urinated on their son's book bag. I thought to myself that I could handle this, but there was this sickening feeling in the pit of my stomach that I had no idea what was to come.

For the first few weeks, she was so hyperactive that I thought I would lose my mind. Every morning she was up at the crack of dawn, although I was used to sleeping until at least 6:30 a.m. She would open up the crate of one of our dogs, let her out, put her back in, let her out, and put her back in again. Then she would run up and down the stairs while calling me literally every five minutes. I counted on one occasion that she called me forty-seven times in one hour, and whenever she asked me for something, she did not want no as an answer. This was no different from any other child, I thought, except for when I said no, she replied, "Do you want me to kill your dog?" I did not know whether to laugh or be scared. It was absolutely unbelievable to hear a child one month shy of being four say such a thing. Another time, I was outside playing with her and she picked a worm up and said, "I love you, little worm" and then forcefully popped it in half. It was disturbing on many levels, but she had probably been told on several occasions that she was loved and then someone hurt her. Every day, I prayed for it to get better, but it seemed to get worse. Each day I was becoming more tired and less patient. I had to get up in the middle of the night to change sheets and scrub the bed because of accidents caused by nightmares. I wised up very soon and bought Pull-Ups and bed padding. I began to resent this child instead of growing close to her. She was consuming all of my time, taking away my sleep, draining me of energy, and begging for food even though we made sure she ate breakfast, lunch, dinner, and three snacks every day like clockwork. The feelings that resided deep inside my heart were not those of a nurturing mother but of a resentful person. I cared for her and continued to help her by trying to provide comfort, but there were days that I did not want to hug her. I just wanted to sleep. Worst of all, no one understood me or the stress I was under. All they saw was a cute little girl. They had no idea what lurked beneath the surface. I was becoming her comfort zone, and I was in for it without knowing how bad it would get.

Tantrums

I remember very clearly going to the grocery store one afternoon with my little four-year-old "bundle of joy." We were about to go in the store, and she wanted to sit inside the carriage where the groceries were to go. I was going to get several items, so she could not sit there. I said very nicely, "Please just sit in the front of the carriage; Mommy has to put groceries in the back." She lost her mind. She threw herself out onto the sidewalk and began to kick and scream at the top of her lungs. Everyone began to stare, and I wanted to hide. Unfortunately, I could not hide, so I just pretended that they were not there and said in a very stern voice, "You will get up right now or we will leave and I will not bring you back to the grocery store with me again." I was as serious as a heart attack. She calmed down a little, so I began to put her in the front of the carriage, but then she started arching her back, which made it difficult to handle her. She sent pain down my back, and I felt like dropping her. I started to place her back in the car and told her we were going to leave if she did not calm down. I guess she wanted to test the waters, because she continued with her tantrums. I closed her door and walked to the other side of the car. By the time I was on the other side, there was nothing left but a wet face. I gently took her out of the car, kissed her, and then put her in the front of the carriage to finally go in the store. Some people might have gone the easy route and just let her get into the back of the carriage, but she was using her behavior to try to control the situation, and she needed to know it wasn't going to work.

On several occasions, we'd be in the car and she would just kick and scream for at least ten minutes. At times, I would stop the car to try to console her, but she would not stop. I would have to turn up the music so that I would not lose my temper. She would get tired of screaming above the music and fall asleep. You know, looking back now, I can see that she was angry. She had lived in four different places and had been in the last one for a year and a half before being placed with us. Each time it had to be a scary feeling to have to leave a home only to be placed with another set of strangers. In spite of knowing this, I knew that if she kept acting out like that, she would have to go see a mental health professional or someone was going to need to get a straitjacket for me.

At home she would bang her head up against the bed and I would have to ignore it as long as it wasn't causing harm to her. In the middle of all this chaos, I had to show her kindness and keep my cool. That was one of the hardest tasks that I have ever had to do: learn to keep my cool in chaotic situations and love no less. Parents, be encouraged. You are not alone.

School

I never thought I would appreciate her going to school so much. I could relax. Preschool helped me keep my sanity. Because of Mary's hyperactivity, when she walked into preschool she could not stay still. She was into everything and had trouble focusing. The other students could relax for periods of time, but she was like a machine. We had to look into sending her to therapy, and their plan was to put her on medication. There were so many incident reports for Mary that it was ridiculous. I had a folder for them. She was constantly getting hurt or hurting someone else. A few times she spit in her friend's face. Later I found out that someone had spit in her face when she was a young toddler. There was always something going on. But school gave me some time to recharge, and she was slowly learning to socialize with others when she wasn't stealing their items. That's a whole other story.

One day I walked into the school hoping that I would get good news for once. Instead I was told that my foster daughter had smeared poop all over the bathroom walls and the toilet. I wanted to spank her and put her in time-out, but the rules said foster children were not to be spanked. I thought this incident would be enough, but no, she had to put it on my walls at home. I was steaming mad, but evidently so was she. Poop smearing can be a sign of rage and anger. On those days I tried to remember that this child had been severely abused, not fed properly, and lacked comfort and love for most of her life. However, that did not mean that I did not still want to give her a country spanking that some folks in the South give you when you don't behave right. I opted out, gave her a bath, threw out her clothes, told her how nasty it was to smear poop on walls, and told her if she did it again, I would take all of her toys and all she would have was a bed to sleep in. And for quite some time, she listened.

The Mucus

I was planning a party for my son. He was turning sixteen, so I wanted him to feel special. Mary did not like for anyone to get attention but her, so this upset her. By the end of the day, I was cleaning up and asked her to go and lie down in her room for a little while. She would not listen, so I picked her up and put her on the bed rather harshly. I needed some time away from her, and the truth is, for once I wanted a day to be about someone else besides her. Despite this, my plan was to clean the house and then go watch a movie with her, because I did not want her to feel left out. When I approached her room, I could not believe my eyes. She had put four huge globs of mucus from her mouth on the blanket. I wanted to throw up, I wanted to lose it, and I wanted her gone. Instead I walked away fuming. I think if I could have spit fire that evening, I would have. I talked myself into calming down and did not say a word to her until I knew I could do so without flipping out. When I was calm enough to talk to her, I did, and then I took the blanket. She could never give me a reason for doing such things so for awhile I stopped asking why. Some of the time I could figure out why. After that moment, I withdrew from her, and every time she acted out with mucus after that incident, it pushed me further away. At times if I did not give her what she wanted or if she did not get all the attention she wanted, she would open her mouth and let spit just drool down her mouth. I did not want her around anymore, and though I knew it was extreme anger, insecurity, and jealousy that had driven her to act this way, I did not care anymore. I just wanted her gone.

The Tongue

When Mary was not getting all the attention she wanted or if anyone was upset with her, she would do very weird things. She wanted attention, yet she did things that made me want to stay away from her as much as possible. On several occasions she would lick things like the couch, the front door, a pole outside, a rock, or anything that was unclean and abnormal to put her mouth on. I had seen other children put their mouths on things during the infant and early toddler stages, but the things she did were just bizarre. She did them not to explore her world but to express anger or a desperate need for the affection she had never received. Sometimes I thought she was near insane. I was unsure if I was able to give her what she needed. I felt like I was trying to make up for everyone who had failed her. One day coming out of therapy she grabbed onto a pole as if to climb it and then licked it with a long stroke. It was disgusting, and every time she'd get mad, out came the tongue. Five minutes later she was telling me, "Mom, I want a hug." I would think to myself, *You just licked a pole like you were crazy and you want a hug. Are you kidding? I want to run from you.* Instead I would give her a hug without allowing myself to be consumed by the emotion. Inside, though, I was getting more and more resentful of her and she was becoming the hell in my life that would not go away.

Cursing

Cooking dinner one evening, I heard my daughter say a curse word. Now, no one in our family cursed, so I knew she had not learned it from us. That was another talk I had to have with her, although she probably would have preferred that I not say anything about it. I could not tolerate a little girl saying bad words. I understood that a potty mouth is a naughty mouth waiting to be popped. My parents would not allow me to curse, and I wasn't going to let my daughter get away with it either. After a while she figured out that it was wrong to use that curse word and graduated to another one. Just picture an adorable little girl who looked like an angel saying things like that. It just did not fit, but neither did the other behaviors. After spending time with her, I felt like cursing, too, but the thoughts were never processed into audible words. Instead I would get upset, scream, and put her in time-out. Repeat! I don't think my screaming helped anyone. I would even get annoyed with myself, but I was so frustrated most of the time—or maybe all of the time—back then. I'm sure my neighbors had to hear me on occasion, so needless to say, I was not being a good Christian example. I was just trying to survive. A line from a popular song goes something like this: "Love lifted me when nothing else would help. Love lifted me."

The problem was that I did not know how to love under these circumstances, and her behavior made me very angry. You know, if I had acted that way as a child because I was angry, I would have gotten the spanking of my life, and then I would have been told to stop crying. There were many times as a child that I wanted to act out because of the things that happened to me, but I could not. I was afraid to, not because my parents were so bad but because my dad and mom expected things to be a certain way. We knew that we'd better obey the rules, so I was not able to express the pain inside my heart for being hurt, which unfortunately included molestation. I just wanted to be a good girl and please everyone so that no one would be upset with me. The few times that my mother caught me doing things that I should not, I wormed my way out of it by trying to be sweet again. I would make up for it later as a teenager, though.

Mary's behavior was bringing up things out of my past that I was not at all comfortable with; I would have much rather not dealt with some of those internal issues. I thought it was better to keep them in the closet than have to deal with them.

Nightmares

Every night for almost a year, Mary wet herself, all because she was having nightmares about "bad guys." These "bad guys" were those she remembered hurting her when she was too little to speak. I told tell her I was sorry someone had hurt her, and I really felt for her in the deepest part of my heart. But I was tired—tired of cleaning urine, poop, and mucus.

A couple of times I took her to my bed with me. She would fall right to sleep, but I would be awakened by the warm feeling of urine on me and my mattress. I would be upset, only to realize I had forgotten to put another Pull-Up on her. It was really hard dealing with a child who was four and a half and wetting the bed every night. Over time it decreased, but there was always something to replace it. She'd fight in her sleep, which I understood, because for years I fought in my sleep. Catch me on a bad night and I'll still try to fight you. Almost every night before bedtime I would give her a hug and read a story from a children's Bible I had bought for her. This seemed to help her fall to sleep quite easily, but we all knew not to wake her up. Naps were pretty much the same. I tried everything to calm her down to take a nap, but she would not do it until I lay beside her or rubbed her back for what seemed like forever. It was sad, really, how much it took to calm her, and for quite some time if I moved, she would grab me back down toward the bed and I would have to wait until she was sound asleep. She'd awake very cranky as if during her sleep she had been somewhere else, and it took about a half hour for her to come out of it. I did not like naptime because it took so much to get her sound asleep, but I knew she needed it, and I needed the time away from her.

The Tics

Apparently mucus, tantrums, nightmares, and tongue issues were not enough. She started having these weird tics. She would blink constantly, make weird coughing noises, and had to touch everything. This child was not a good match for me, but I still cared about her. I looked up tics in relation to ADHD (attention deficit hyperactivity disorder) symptoms, and sure enough there was a relationship for some individuals. I didn't know if she had ADHD or severe anxiety or maybe even both, but there were also definitely developmental delays, among other problems. The doctors seemed to think she suffered from both. The problems seemed unceasing. Those tics annoyed me to no end. She could not stay still, focus, or stay on task, and the list continued on. The short-term medication calmed her down for a few hours but did not seem to help the other issues. Whenever she would start those tics, I wanted to make her stop, but there was nothing I could do. *Oh God!* I thought, *what have you given to me?*

I felt sorry for her, but I was also annoyed by her. The sad thing is that as I write this, I feel bad for having felt that way, but it is the truth: I was annoyed with all of her problems.

The Social Workers

I knew that the social workers were just doing their jobs, but I saw them every week when Mary first came and then every other week after about a month or two. It seemed that they visited too often.

I really did not look forward to the visits, because although Mary would be on her best behavior while they were there, she would act out when they left. Initially she was scared that they would take her out of another home, and who could blame her? Oftentimes when the doorbell rang, she would go running like a maniac throughout the house, the dogs would start barking, and I would feel hopeless. The social workers would sit and talk to her or to me while watching our interaction. It felt weird for a while. One of them was really good at listening to the issues we were facing, but she could not do much except offer advice. There was nothing she could really do to make Mary act right, although if she could have, I'm sure she would have. The other social worker from the state was nice, but I did not feel as if I could talk to her about anything. I think she dealt with so many negative things on her job that she probably did not want to hear any more. They did not know it, but every time they came in, it felt like a disruption in our lives. It was a reminder that Mary was not really ours and that her problems were deep; otherwise we would not have two social workers coming to see us. She was not a normal child, and the sacrifice it took to schedule mandatory visits with social workers, speech therapists, and mental health specialists was a bit much. In addition to that, I was working at a children's hospital part-time, going to school to be an RN part-time, and trying to run a nonprofit I had started in 2003. The insanity of it all was driving me up a wall. So I took a year off from school to raise Mary. I resented having to do this, but I did it anyway.

Condemnation

Oh, people can be very judgmental. Not many would take in a foster child, but there are many who will critique and judge everything you do. If we had enough parents out there for children, social workers would not have casework overloads. There would not be children without permanent homes. It'd be nice if the biological parents could care for them so that foster care wasn't needed in the first place, but we live in a world where things are often not as they should be.

I frequently felt like people were watching us, especially when they knew Mary was a foster child. It would make me so angry. Instead of getting encouragement, I would get glares and disparagement. My husband was better at dealing with this because he never really cared what others thought. I was raised to be a people-pleaser. Every time someone would stare at us, I would feel uncomfortable and think, *What did I do wrong now?* I would allow people to make me feel as if they could do a better job, because when they spent a little time with her, she did not act out. They did not understand that foster children often act out with those individuals who are the closest to them because they are often testing boundaries and security. Many times they feel the new set of parents will send them away as well, and when you don't, it becomes scary. So they behave in a manner that often pushes you away, even though it is the opposite of what they need and want. They may often produce what they fear the most: being abandoned. It is difficult, but it is familiar. I could not lecture people on the trials and tribulations of foster parenting if they had never been in that situation. They just would not get it, and I would have expended energy that I simply did not have. So I just let them think what they wanted. It burned me up, but there was nothing I could do but move on. It's really funny how many people would not make a move to attempt the challenges that we took on, yet they sat back and found everything wrong. You should never judge anyone until you have walked in their shoes. I desperately wanted things to be different, but they were not and this is how I felt ...

Help Me Fight

This cloud upon me is like death at my door,
and I cannot enter into the presence of the Lord.
I am consumed by agony and frustration,
and every time I move to do right, I get more aggravated.

There is a lot of pain in my life and I don't know
why it comes and where it comes from.
It just comes over me so bad
that I feel like crying and then dying.
I want to give up.

I don't recognize this person; she is cruel and lost.
She is mean and distraught.
Who can console her?
Who can feel her pain?

No one.

There is no one to talk to.

I don't like her,

but when she comes around, she is comfortable and familiar.

She is smiling but aching.

She is laughing but crying,

and no one understands her pain.

She cannot expect them to.

She knows better than to trust those around her.

They say be yourself, but they would not if they knew how tragic

things were.

If I walked around expressing the way I feel

I would tell anyone and everyone to get out of my face.

And the ones that I love I would warn them of my pain.

I would tell them that it hurts,

and though my intention is not to hurt the ones I love,

it would be inevitable.

Who can heal me?

Where is God?

It's all out there now.

Do you still love me?

Or do you now judge me?

Oh, fellow people of my sad world,

do you understand?

Do you see that I am trying?

Trying to live but dying,

Trying to give but not surviving,

Hating when I want to love,

Looking above but feeling there is no hope for me.

Yes, the words I speak are depressing, but they are the words of many
who dare not speak
because they have to work.
They have families.
They want others not to reject them, so they act as if it's okay
until they are alone.
Then they are popping pills, smoking, drinking
and trying desperately to make it go away.
But it won't. It just won't leave.
It's depression.
It wants you all to itself.

I pray and I pray to stay, and I hear in my heart,
"Will you fight to be free or will you be consumed by it?
No doubt about it, this life can be hard
But will you fight?"
And I say,
"I want to fight.
I need to fight.
Help me, God, to fight, please!"

Exhaustion

I was tired of my life, my new child, and the little support I received. My mother was probably one of the few people who initially seemed to understand how I felt, and my dad did often try praying with me, for me and for Mary. It is probably the rock that helped us all survive. But even they had their limitations, and after a while I am sure that they did not want to hear about the next problem, or at least it appeared that way. During this time, I had a friend in whom I confided, but sooner rather than later, it appeared that as much as she tried, she did not really understand either, and so I was left feeling alone. My husband was at work most of the time, so Mary was my responsibility the majority of the time. She drained me in every sense of the word, and it was getting harder and harder not to resent her. I prayed and cried. I prayed and cried some more, and then I stopped praying and just *got mad*!

I said to God, "I wanted to help a child, I wanted a child, I asked for a child, and this is what you give me. This crazy nut—she brings out the worst in me. I have to deal with parts of myself that I am not comfortable dealing with, and these judgmental people are getting on my nerves. She has to go, and I know it will hurt us all, but sooner or later we will get over it. What was I thinking bringing her here?"

I Don't Want to Get Out of Bed

There were many days that I just did not want to get out of bed. I wanted to sleep and not wake up. The morning sun became an irritant, along with my daughter making noise on purpose to awake me from my sleep. I just did not want the morning to come. *If only I could sleep forever*, I thought, or *Maybe I can run away from my life*. I loved sleep. I did not have to think, solve problems, worry, get frustrated, or deal with any crazy behaviors. I did not have to think about the pain that lurked inside of me. At times I had bad dreams, but it was better than dealing with reality. Reality was too difficult for me, and I hated it. No one could soothe my soul during this time. I would pray mostly to get out my aggression and to ask for solutions, but none ever seemed to come. Maybe I should say none that I wanted to come. Everywhere I went, there was a message about loving difficult people. I did not even love myself, so how in the world could I love a difficult person to the extent that she needed? Some days I wished that my daughter would not come near me or even look at me. I did not want to see her face. It reminded me of stress and how much I wanted to be what she needed but couldn't be. Quite honestly, it made me feel better that the foster moms before me could not handle her either, because that meant I wasn't a failure. And my God, if her own biological mother did not keep her, I could not be that bad. My thoughts were so misconstrued. On the other hand, I felt anguish about her early beginnings, because I knew this lack of security had produced many problems within her. My emotions were all over the place.

Early on, my husband and I had to take foster-parenting classes so we would be prepared for the behaviors we would have to deal with. One of the things we learned was that many of these children would display roller-coaster behaviors, which would in turn make the parents feel the same at times. Oh my! How true it came to be. I was naive to think that just providing a safe home and a little love would instantly do the trick. Even though I heard what the social workers said, I had believed that it would be okay the moment we embraced our foster child. I wanted a perfect family, and I found out quite quickly that it does not exist.

Sometimes, I set myself up for failure without realizing it. I had unreasonable expectations. I wanted a child who had lived in four homes by the age of four to come into my house and be a normal child. And when she was not, I resented her and myself for bringing her in. I felt at one point that I had destroyed my peaceful home because of her. My son once said to me that maybe I was not cut out to have more than one child. I thought about what he said and even came to the conclusion that maybe he was right, but I did not have the heart to send her away. I thought it was unfair for a child to be tossed around and have no security, but keeping her sent me into a deep depression, and I simply just wanted to sleep it away.

Losing My Cool

I had had enough, and no one understood. I would try to tell people what I was going through without going into detail, and they just would not get it. Mary was cute, and I was the big, bad, stressed-out mommy. They would say, "It will be okay" or some would just remain judgmental as if they were the foster-parent jury. Meanwhile she was driving me insane. There were days when I would just lose it and scream at the top of my lungs at her. I just could not tolerate her anymore. I felt at the time that she was destroying my life. My relationship with my husband was becoming strained. I was always cranky, and my husband was working fifty hours per week and he was cranky. And my goodness, she would not stop calling me. One day she just kept calling me over and over and asking me for something that I had said no to on several occasions. I slammed my hand on the counter and screamed, "No! And would you please leave me alone?" Well, of course I felt bad, but it was one of the few times she listened. It was probably because she was scared, but nevertheless she left me alone for at least a half hour.

Therapy for Her

Therapy started about eight months after she entered into our care. Once again the therapist remarked how cute she was and that we dressed her so cute. And I thought to myself, *You have no idea. Don't you know that crazy people can come in cute packages?* My thoughts in those days were running like crazy. Every week, I faithfully took her to therapy. She was put on medication, which helped to calm her. Now at least I could get through to her mind. For months I had toyed with the idea of medication. I felt so bad about her having to be medicated, but I knew that if they did not medicate her, I would be in a straitjacket or she would have to go. And I knew that if she left, the progress that she had made would be lost, so I agreed to put her on the lowest dose possible for a short while. It's not like I had much of a choice once the state and the doctors decided it was what she needed, but I guess I was considered part of the therapeutic treatment team for her. It calmed her down in about thirty minutes and lasted for three hours. It was long enough to make her stable so she was teachable and long enough to help me hold on to my sanity. Some time ago, I had remarked to an individual that I thought it was wrong to put children on medication for hyperactivity, impulsiveness, and focusing problems, but it was not until I experienced the difficulty of raising a child with clinical diagnoses that I realized I had spoken out of ignorance. And though I still firmly believe that no medication should be misused or abused, there are children who have such severe problems that it often seems that medication may be the only avenue to a more normal way of life.

I hoped mental health therapy helped her but never really knew for sure. However, I knew we were desperate for help, so we tried everything that was made available.

Therapy for Me

I started calling psychologists, psychiatrists, and anyone I thought could help. I was feeling as if I were going to lose it. At this point Mary had started to make a little progress. She was wetting the bed and stealing only a few times per month. She was no longer smearing poop. She was less hyperactive, and because of this she was focusing better in school. I had spent more than a year loving this uncontrollable child, and now I was feeling out of control.

After about six weeks of looking, I was able to find a mental health professional who could help me deal with the emotions that were resurfacing from my own past. It was costly, but it was better to pay than to go *crazy*! I never quite understood this man, who would sit and listen while offering very little feedback. He looked more depressed than me. Often I found myself filling in where he should have been, but I figured he knew what he was doing. I started talking about the abuse that had happened in my childhood after about three visits. I had no idea how angry I was with my parents for not protecting me. I was angry with myself for not being able to stand up and speak. I was angry with the man who molested me, and mostly I was mad at God for his lack of intervention to help me or all the other children who had been hurt by people. Where was he? My anger began to come out in my words. I no longer had a guard on my mouth after this point. I just spoke what I felt, and in my mind I did not care who was in my way. If they hurt me, it was over. If they said something I did not like, I would say something back to hurt them more, and no one was off limits.

When people violate you, it can leave you feeling helpless, angry, bitter, and unexplainably sad inside. A child has no defense against an adult except to tell another adult, and when you look for help but instead get no help, a change occurs in your mind. Trust is gone, and often it will be difficult to trust anyone for a very long time, if ever.

Imagine a baby being abused. Where is their voice? My daughter, Mary, was abused, and her voice could not be heard except through her tears. When she cried, she was beaten more. This was my connection with her that no one else seemed to understand. I felt a lot of the feelings she was feeling, but at the same time I was resentful that her behavior was making these feelings come alive in me again.

Every week I showed up at these appointments, and in the middle of it all, we decided we would adopt her. God only knows how we managed to come to this conclusion in the middle of chaos. She was slowly getting better, and although we hoped it would continue, I felt as if I were getting worse. I was short-tempered. I did not want to socialize with anyone, and every day I had to pick Mary up from school. Looking at her reminded me of what was not right in my life. I would take her to the park after school so she could expend some energy and I wouldn't be left so tired. I also wanted her to have good memories of playing at the park and being happy. Still, just thinking of the things that were floating in my mind was exhausting, and I felt as if I wanted to literally die. I did not want to be hugged by my daughter—or anyone, for that matter, who would drain any energy from me. Some people give when they hug, and others take. I barely had enough for myself.

I tried to keep her occupied so she would not notice the lack of affection I was releasing. Now, of course, anyone who has had a child who requires constant affection and attention knows that this method did not work for long. She would get fussy and needy. So I did things like reading books, blowing kisses, and tucking her in at night. This would help me feel like she was not taking all of my energy, because I had very little to survive on.

Tackling these issues in therapy was not easy, and at the same time I was trying to protect everyone's privacy. After a while, I just figured I would not get better if I did not spill everything I was feeling. It always felt weird when I walked in the door of the rather gloomy office surrounded my medical books that did not look like they had been used for quite some time, but I kept going because it was a way to release stress and have a nonjudgmental person listen to me. I found out a lot more about myself. I did not trust anyone, not even myself. I loved my parents, but I was angry with them for sweeping the abuse under the rug and hoping it would just go away. I was angry with my husband for not understanding me, though I barely understood myself, and for being so cruel in the early part of our relationship. I was disappointed in friends in my life, and the more I talked, the more I ached inside, because I realized that there were some ugly things inside of me as well.

Most of my early life, I had grown up in church, faithfully serving God until later I realized I was faithfully serving people. I loved the Lord even in my anger because deep down inside, I knew that he loved me and that he was not the problem—humans were. I just did not understand why he allowed so much pain in the world and why he allowed such turmoil in my life.

In my teenage years, I rebelled like I was part of the Great Rebellion. I ran way from home just shy of being sixteen years old, only to find trouble on the other side. I ran right into the same type of man who had molested me. This grown man told me he was nineteen, although later I found out he was twenty-eight years old. He stole what virginity I had left through his deception and lies. He said that he loved me and wanted me. Soon afterward, I stopped going to school and was not eating properly. As a matter of fact, I remember going three days without eating at all, and toward the end of the third day he bought me a can of pasta from the corner convenience store. He knew I had no money, food, or transportation, and stupid me thought he was actually trying to take care of me. It was more like he fed me before I died. He continued to tell me that he loved me, but he was raping my mind and body without my having a clue of the damage that was being done. He told me that he had a BMW and was going to take me to California, where he was going to become a singer. He also told me that he had money and had gold displayed all over his room. All lies. The gold was fake. It actually turned green when he allowed me to wear a necklace. There was only one real piece of gold jewelry, and someone stole it from me. The BMW was just a picture of a car that he had found in a book. He sold a dream to my naïve mind. It's amazing what impresses the young mind of someone who is so desperate to be wanted. And quite frankly, there was nothing good looking about this man, and I mean absolutely nothing. But when he said, "I love you," I ignored all of that. Unfortunately, I found out how deceptive he was after he violated me and I became pregnant. As I mentioned before, I was rarely fed, and at five and a half months pregnant I lost the baby. The umbilical cord strangled the baby and he probably was too weak to fight. I was definitely malnourished and had lost a significant amount of weight. I did not know from a medical perspective if the lack of food had caused the baby to die, but this was a horrible part of my life that caused a lot of pain. I had to go into the hospital to have my labor induced, but before that I had to go home over the weekend knowing that the baby had already died inside of me. So from Friday to Monday I felt numb. By that time an infection had already started to develop in my system, so instead of spending a night in the hospital, I was there for almost a week.

As my labor was induced, I told the nurse that I was going into labor, but she did not believe me. She told me it would take a little bit longer, and boy, was she wrong. Drugged up from medication and hooked up to an IV, I walked to the bathroom, where my poor lifeless child was born in the toilet. I screamed, and the nurses came in with disbelief on their faces. This is not the end of this horrific story. My baby was put in blankets so that I could hold him, and then I was asked, "Would you like to have us dispose of the baby, or would you like to have your own burial and funeral service?" I wanted so bad to have my own service and a place that I could visit my child when I needed to, but I knew my parents could not afford it and the baby's father had never bothered to show up. He called and that was it. He probably was afraid of going to jail. I always regretted that decision, the decision that I made for my baby. He deserved a tombstone. My soul has regretted that decision, and yet I had to continue on. Each traumatic incident in my life broke my spirit more.

These children in foster care have broken spirits, and some of them act out because they feel unloved, unwanted, and pushed aside. I began to understand that the purpose for my existence in life might be to help heal the broken-hearted through the love of God, but there would be a long road to get there. My difficult child would help me open up the old wounds so that I could deal with them. In the process, I would be healed and so would she, but it would be an exhausting journey.

As I mentioned before, there are many judgmental people in this world, and many times it's their own insecurities or self-righteous attitude that produces these reactions. The truth is, you can't really expect them to understand. Only those of us who have endured great pain and come through it can truly empathize with those who are hurting. And even then the wounded must be healed before they can even show true love to those who so desperately need it.

Relapse

At this point Mary's behavior had improved a little. She was interacting with her peers better, and the acting out was not as bad for a while. Unfortunately, the good behavior never seemed to last long. I picked her up from school three days in a row when she had stolen something from somebody. She was learning to be good at it. One day we were in the store and she stole lip gloss. I did not realize it, of course, until we arrived at home, so I put her back into the car and drove all the way back to the store and made her apologize. I would not let the lady tell her it was okay, because it was not. It was getting to the point where she would steal from school, home, and other people's houses. For a while, taking her back to the store seemed to work. Then one day the earrings and pearl necklace that I could not find showed up in her closet. I knew that she was taking things to feel secure, because when she first came to live with us, she took my husband's money out of his wallet, took our son's Game Boy, and took my toothbrush. These were all very personal items, and she was trying to hold on to them for fear of losing her new family. So we started giving her personal items. I bought her a necklace, and my husband let her sleep in his shirt at night. Our son wanted no part of it, so we just gave him back his items. In addition, we told her that if she kept stealing, she would end up in jail when she was older. To make her understand, I drove her to the police station. I told her that if you are a good girl, the cops protect you and keep you safe, but if you steal, they put you in jail. It may seem a bit harsh for a five-year-old child, but the situation was getting out of control, and so was she. I did not know what to do. My way of thinking at the time was, *Better to see the police station now as a visit than to spend time behind bars later as a home.* If a broken child grows to be a young adult and continues the same behavior, he or she cannot say to an arresting officer, "I have emotional problems and an attachment disorder and that is why I steal" and expect the cop to let them go. It's not reality. I don't think it was the best way to handle it—it can produce fear—but it was all I felt I had at the time. I really feared for her future, because I could honestly see her being locked up very early in life.

Hoarding Food

One morning I awoke to find crumbs in Mary's bed from cookies. Later it was doughnuts. I had to clean the bed, and I learned to put everything away that I did not want her to get to the night before. When children are not given proper nutrition, they take food and hide it because they are afraid they will not be fed. Food can also be comforting to them. We provided her with meals every day on schedule so that she would learn that she could depend on us to feed her, but old habits aren't so easily broken. Early in her life, adults were not dependable, and it would take some time to show her differently.

Of all the hoarding and attempts to steal food, the peanut butter episode was the worst. The smell of peanut butter was throughout the house, and I had never smelled peanut aroma like that before. I followed the smell and guess where it came from— Mary's room. She had peanut butter all over herself. She had taken her hand and covered it with peanut butter and was just sucking on it desperately. I have never seen anything like it in my life. It was not like a child who had gotten her hands in the "cookie jar." Peanut butter was on her shirt, on the bed, and on her face. It was sickening. A while later, I began to try to figure out if there was a trigger for the behavior. I felt like I may have been partly to blame for that incident, because the day before I had lost my temper with her. I had grabbed her by her clothes while telling her I was sick and tired of her not listening and acting like she was out of her mind.

Well, she was out of her mind at the time. There were times that she would just space out and not be responsive. Noises like pots, knocking on doors, or even the closing of a door would send her into a frenzy. Sometimes, I did not know what to do, but jacking her up sure wasn't the answer. I think these actions reminded her of previously being in a scary house where she had no food and was beaten. My goal was to help heal her, but sometimes I did not feel like a healer but just a survivor of a situation I did not feel equipped for. And many times no matter what I did, she'd still be a force that was out of control. After the peanut butter incident, we talked to her to remind her of the meals that we gave her every day. I would say, "We will feed you. Please don't worry." I also apologized later for losing my temper with her. After some time passed, the hoarding did not happen often, and the peanut butter episode never happened again. She did, however, do meal checks to remind herself what was coming next. It was annoying but better than the alternative.

Use Wisdom

There is no way to save every child, but if you do decide to help a child or children, be wise. Many times I was not. Some children will not work out in your home. Their problems may exceed your limitations, so be aware of your limitations. Unfortunately, I found out mine during the process. Get as much information as you can from the social workers. Don't be afraid to ask questions. It's your life that is changing, not theirs, and if you have a good social worker, he or she will try to help you, not withhold important information. My husband gave me advice along the way that I should have listened to. He said, "Wait: you are in school, which will make it harder for you." He also said, "It won't be as easy as you think." Both statements were true, but I felt this great desire to help a child, and I proceeded without caution. I do not regret making the decision to bring her into our home. I do regret not being wiser about the timing and the effect that it would have on all of our lives.

It's a wonderful thing to have the heart to help someone, but carefully analyze the behaviors that are tolerable and the ones that are not for you and your family. Some you will not know until later, but again, be wise.

Asthma

Mary also has asthma, which was really bad during the fall and winter seasons. One night I awoke to her gasping and coughing. Before she went to bed, I had heard slight wheezing, but I had hoped it would go away. And wouldn't you know, after all the days and nights that I had responsibly left one pump at home and one at school, I had left them both at her school. I had to drive over to my mom's house at 1:30 a.m. to get an asthma pump. Thank God my mom was less than ten minutes away. I gave Mary the asthma treatment as directed by the doctor every three hours, and the symptoms subsided. Fortunately, she did not have to go to the hospital, though we came pretty close to taking her. The next morning was the only morning she slept late, but I was exhausted as ever. If I had not provided care to asthma patients before her asthma attack that night, I would have been scared.

We had a few more of these episodes over time, and each time became easier to deal with. I tried to keep her as healthy as possible to avoid any respiratory problems. Her biological family history revealed that a few other people had asthma, so we knew she might not grow out of it.

Holidays

I remember the first Christmas that Mary was with us. It was tough for her, because during that time she remembered holidays at her previous foster family's house. She'd sing little songs about her old family, but every time I'd ask her if she wanted to visit them, she'd say, "No!" So I did not talk about it unless she wanted to. For at least a year and a half they would send her things for Christmas, Easter, and her birthday. It made Mary smile, but she still had no desire to see them, so after a while she did not speak of them so frequently. When she wanted, I'd call them so she could say hello, but I'd do it only if she desired, so she'd have some control. Sometimes the reason foster children are so combative is that they have been out of control for so long and try to regain control of their environment with negative behavior. It has to be hard for children to be in a home and know individuals as family and then one day no longer be in that family. Even if the family was not good for them, an attachment still occurs. Memories are there, and it takes time to make new memories. If at all possible during the hectic time of getting adjusted to having a new, difficult child in the home, make the memories as precious and special as possible. If you mess up from time to time, it's okay to apologize for your mistakes. The child will not see you as this perfect person they have to live up to but as a human who is flawed with a heart kind enough to say "I'm sorry."

I'm the Child, You're the Mommy

I knew I was hard on Mary sometimes, but at times it was the only way I felt I could get her to listen. I did not want her to completely feel out of control, so we would play a game called I'm the Child, You're the Mommy. She would pretend to be the mommy and put me in time-out for something I did wrong. She had so much fun telling me what to do. She used it to her advantage too. While I was pretending to be the child, she'd make me clean her room. I knew what she was doing, but I cleaned it anyway. I was kind of impressed that she was smart enough to have me clean the room during play so that she would not have to clean it later. She'd say to me, "Be quiet and listen or you'll go in time-out," and I would respond in her manner by hopping up and down, crying and throwing a tantrum. She'd then tell my husband on me and he would say, "Take her toys and put her in time-out." Inside I was laughing because she would get so serious. We'd play this for about a half hour or so until I was tired of being in time-out, and then I became Mommy again. Little things like that can help a child feel less defenseless. Child or adult, no one likes to be told what to do all the time without having any control.

A Lot of Work, Small Results

At times I felt that I put so much work into trying to get Mary to be better that it was not rewarding at all when she made slight progress. I wanted more. I thought to myself, *Doesn't this child know how I gave up my life to give her a good home?* And quite honestly, I felt like she owed me more than good behavior once in a while. I did not say I was right for feeling this way, but it's what I felt. Some would comment that she had made a lot of progress, but in my eyes she was a problem child and the rate at which she was making progress was not quick enough. I spoke to one of the social workers about her behavior, and she responded by saying, "True change does not happen overnight. It takes time, and if it happens too quickly, don't trust it." She was right, but I was sick and tired of trying to get orange juice out of a lemon.

I kept trying, even though everything inside of me was telling me to give up. Thoughts would come into my mind that were not so pleasant. I wanted to give her up. I wanted her out of my life. I kept saying to my husband, "Now I see why the other families gave her up." But there was something deep inside my heart that would not let me turn this child away. Some might call it compassion, but I knew I had no more compassion to give. My compassion bank was drained and overdrawn. And I believe to this day that God helped me to not give up because he wanted this child's life to be saved and in the middle of it, I would be taught how to love unconditionally. I did not want to love unconditionally, because too many people had hurt me starting very early in my life. As time went on, many people I allowed myself to get close to left me. I felt no one loved me unconditionally. I was expected to be a certain way to receive affection, and if I was not, I was disposable. The ironic thing is that I knew this, but I kept being attracted to those sorts of people—the type who expected me to be perfect and showered me with praise until I fell short of their expectations. It's a sad way to live, and I began to think maybe I was expecting my daughter to perform in the same manner. But how could she? She had no previous structure, no kindness, no love, and only minimal food, and she had been beaten like a rag doll by her abusers. After resolving this in my mind, I tried very hard to expect less of her until her heart was mended from her past. It was hard to do this—very hard—and with little support I could not do it as much as I wanted.

Shutting Them Out

For a while, I wanted to shut everybody out. I wanted to have a drink even though I had not had a drink in years. I was never an alcoholic, but after committing myself to God, I just did not drink anymore. The urges would come and I would say, "God, please help me; I know this is not the way to deal with problems." Somehow, I would get some strength not to return to my old way of thinking. My doctor thought of putting me on Valium to calm my nerves. My nerves were a wreck, and I had few coping mechanisms left. I refused to go on medication, so I went back to the old faithful coping mechanism: I shut people out from my heart and my emotions and just lived life without feeling for a few weeks. It didn't last long. The problem with acting in this manner is that it is not who I truly am, so when I acted this way, it just made me more miserable. It was all I felt that I had left at the time. I was feeling misunderstood, with very little love being given to my spirit, and yet people were taking it out like it was free gas. I stopped them from draining me by shutting them out. There is a balance. No one should be allowed to drain your spirit with neediness and negative behavior, but there is nothing wrong with loving, either, without expecting the same degree of love. You cannot make someone love you, but in a healthy relationship, respect and reasonable boundaries are important. However, it is hard to find a balance with feelings of resentment and hurt. I was trying so hard to be tough and not care. It didn't feel good, but it felt safe, so for a while when I was overwhelmed, I'd just shut 'em out.

Somebody Take Care of Me

By this time one of my best friends was married and consumed with married life, and I felt like yesterday's news. Who knows, maybe I was, but I knew I had no one to take care of me or to talk to. My husband was still working more than fifty hours a week, and when he came home, he was exhausted and cranky. I could not seem to do anything right for him except feed him, and even then, the food sometimes didn't have enough pepper or salt. I had flashes of hitting him with a frying pan, but I did not want to end up on the show *Snapped*, so I tried my hardest not to snap and maintain sanity. I also knew it was hard to work eleven-hour days and have to commute for almost an hour each way. He needed time to breathe and relax as did I, but for different reasons. I wanted to take my stress out on someone, so I took it out on myself. I would call myself stupid or an idiot for any mistake I made. When I did something wrong, I punished myself for days, weeks, months, and my heart might even say years. I reminded myself that he worked hard every day to take care of us and that even though I did not get to spend a lot of time with him, I knew that he loved me. People who have been abused need constant reassurance until they feel safe. The only place I felt safe was in the arms of God, and I had not talked to him in quite some time because I was angry. I wanted God to be proud of me so I tried to do everything right, but I failed to realize that he loved me even when I did wrong. I knew he did not agree with sin because I had been told it since I was a young child. The problem was that my thinking was not clear. I had been abused physically, verbally, and sexually by different people, so I had to be wrong at just about everything. I figured something had to be wrong with me if people kept hurting me this way. This was incorrect, but of course I did not know that in my mind and heart. I wanted to live, and I mean really live, but I could not because inside I was dying a slow death. There were so many issues that never seemed to go away.

What Is Love?

My son was a teenager and was growing further away from me. I had loved my son so much; he had been my only child for fifteen years. He had been such a joy to me, and I felt as if I was losing him. I felt I was losing everything that had brought me joy and it was being replaced my chaos and mayhem. He was growing up and seemed to resent me, but the love I felt for him never wavered. I wanted to love Mary the way I loved my son, but there was no biological bond and it's hard to bond when a child repulses you with his or her behavior. I felt bad about it every day, but I kept trying. I tried to look at her cute little face and how peaceful she looked when she was sleeping. It worked at times, and on the days when she was doing okay, I tried to bond with her without letting her smother me. Everyone deserves love, but it felt as if the love that I gave was damaged. People in my life were good at draining my spirit, or maybe I was good at letting them. In spite of this, I longed for the day when someone would look beyond my protective demeanor, love me, hug me without looking for something, and never let me go. I quickly reminded myself that this was impossible, because every living being would die one day and no one could offer perfect love but God.

What is love anyway? Is it emotion? Is it sweaty palms and heated nights? Is it poetry in the ear of a woman who has never heard it from a man? Is it committing to one partner for the rest of your life? Or is it the unconditional way in which we give kindness, forgiveness, patience, affection, and understanding to one another? Ever find it difficult to forgive and love those who have hurt you? Well, I have. I have even wanted to forgive them, but the lump stays in my throat and the knot stays in my heart while the heaviness of not forgiving lies and waits for the next attack so that it can grow into bitterness and then hatred. Listen, you can't heal or love unconditionally until you are truthful with yourself. One minute I have felt affection for people and the next I have felt like taking them for a long ride in the countryside with only me returning.

I felt I had given so much affection that I wanted love back, and that if I couldn't get it, everybody needed to go, including Mary. But then out of the blue, she'd say, "Mom, I love you. You're the best mom ever." I'd think to myself, *Is she for real?* I thought I was doing a poor job and that she could not possibly love someone she had known for such a short time, but every time I would tell her I loved her, she'd say, "I know." And I suppose she did know, because every time I watched her sleep, my heart was overwhelmed with affection, and I knew I did not really want to give her up. I just needed to be cared for, and I needed her behavior to change.

Growing in My Heart

Somewhere along the way, I decided that I would try harder to understand Mary even if I did not receive the same understanding from people around me. I questioned myself often, asking if I could really care for her for the rest of my life. Could I? Should I? And would I be crazy if I did? What would others think? Would they continually critique me? Would they approve? Would my family ever adjust to the chaos? So many questions, so many appointments, so many workers, so much school, so much work, so little sleep, so little fun, so little quiet time. Was I really out of mind, taking on this responsibility? My husband had warned me. Was he right and was it too late to turn back after the fact? Would she be okay if she had to go away? I decided to find out. I asked Mary how she would feel if she had to go live with some other really nice people. I would not advise asking a foster child that question if it can be avoided, but I was desperate and wanted to know if her reaction would be extreme or maybe she'd be okay. When she first came to us, she never shed a tear about her previous foster family, although I am sure she missed them, because from time to time she would talk about them. I thought maybe she'd be fine the fifth time around. It's amazing the things that one can convince him- or herself of when one is trying to get out of an experience without feeling guilty. Well, she responded with sadness and tears. She proceeded to tell me that I was her mom, my husband was her dad, my son was her brother, and the dogs would miss her. She also said that the other people wouldn't be nice and that she loved her room. I felt so bad, but did I feel bad enough to parent her for the rest of her life? I decided that day that the decision that we made about her future would be based not on guilt but on love. I would hate myself later if I did it because of guilt. But every time I was ready to give up, I would think of that moment.

Change Things Around

After being tired for so long, I decided to change some things around. When she was a toddler, I had put Mary to bed at 8:00 p.m. Since she was older, I decided I would make 8:00 p.m. bath time to help relax her. At about 8:30 p.m., I combed her hair, had her brush her teeth, read her a book or let her watch a show on the Disney Channel for a little while. Bedtime was 9:00 p.m., and she'd fall asleep before 9:15 p.m. This still gave me time to make lunch for the next day, study for a little bit, and get in bed by 11:00 p.m. or so. By changing the time a little, she would sleep until about 7:00 a.m. and still get the amount of rest she needed. This was a better time for everyone in the house, though it appeared to be a minimal change. It took a while to change things, but we were a little more rested to deal with stress, and she was just fine.

I consistently continued to remind her every day of her meals and sometimes let her help me prepare them. This way she wasn't annoying me every five minutes for food and she felt more secure. If we went on a trip, I put a snack in her bag so she could decide when she wanted it. At times I would also give her a toy from home so she would not feel the need to steal. I made a lot of changes, including how I reacted to her behavior. When she had a tantrum, I would ignore it. When she spit, I would say, "Go look at yourself in the mirror and then wipe your mouth" and soon she started to get it. One time one of our dogs was really sick because she was overeating and trying to take the other dog's food plus her own. I remarked, "Wow, look at what happened to the dog because she did not want to share." Mary understood, and I did not have to say it directly to her. Every time the dog would try to take the other dog's food, she'd say to her, "You'd better not be greedy or you will get sick." I was as careful as possible in handling that situation because I did not want her to be overly conscious of food, but I also did not want her to overeat. To this day, she can probably eat as much as my husband or me, but she does not beg for food as much after she has eaten, and she understands when she is full. Initially, she was eating for emotional reasons, because the food made her feel good. Unfortunately, this problem extends way beyond the arena of abused children.

Things did not get better overnight, but they did get better. The problems did not stop completely, but they were not as frequent. That was an accomplishment. I began to think that maybe this could be done. Maybe!

The Sun Begins to Shine

A few times Mary told me that she was an angel and that God had told her to come to us. I would say to myself, *If she is an angel, she is a crazy angel.*

I would also say inwardly, *Why did God have to send me the crazy angel? He has so many angels, and there are already enough crazy people and things in my life.* The fact of the matter was that I did love her with all of the craziness, and at times she began to be sweet. She'd come to my bed in the morning and tell me I was beautiful and that I was the best mom. Then I knew she had to be telling the truth when she said that she loved me, because back then in the morning at 6:45 a.m. I barely felt alive let alone looked alive. There began to be more days that she was not wetting the bed, having tantrums, yelling out, and whatever else floated her boat. Finally, the sun was beginning to shine.

Starting the Adoption Process

Paperwork. I do not like paperwork, yet it consumes by life. The counter has it, the mail slots have it, and I cannot get out from underneath it. I even started collecting e-mails. But there was more to come. We were planning to adopt Mary. My husband did not have the heart to give her up, and neither did I. A part of me did not want to keep her, because I feared not being able to handle her. I feared her relapses, but the other part of me won, as it often does.

First each person in the house had to get a physical, as if the physical the year before wasn't enough. Part of the physical consisted of getting blood work done. Then we had to get the doctor to sign the forms, saying that we were healthy and capable of adopting. One would think that the process would go simply, but it did not. It took six weeks to get the paperwork signed. In addition to the blood work, drug tests were done. Mary had been in our house for more than a year and a half, and still it was as if we were starting from scratch. I often wondered if it was really worth it. I wondered if she would ever appreciate it. I wondered if after all the work I put in for her she would one day still want to find her biological mother. I was scared to get close to her because of her emotional issues and because I feared that one day she would leave me for a woman who had tossed her aside as if she did not matter. My thoughts were somewhat selfish but very honest and even valid. All of these things crowded my mind. I did not sleep well and was very apprehensive about walking into something I could not get myself out of. My husband always said I was constantly looking for the next thing to do, and maybe I had gone too far this time. Who was I to think that I could bring a stranger into our home and love her as if she had been born to us? Who was I to do such a thing? And if I did, would I live to regret it?

After getting all the paperwork together and getting three references from friends and family, we submitted it all and waited. During those days I thought of every reason to back out, but I just could not do it. Was it possible that she was meant to be our child? Could such a thing happen? Could it be that children who are neglected and abused have other families who are meant to be their family? Did she really love me or was she just desperate for anyone's affection? Often it seemed that it did not matter who gave her attention or loved her, just as long as she could thrive off of it. I wanted my own birthed child so that the relationship would be more secure. Weren't all my children supposed to be biologically mine? I began to resent my husband for our not being pregnant, and thought that if she had just been born to me, everything would have been fine. He constantly reminded me that I was the one who wanted to help this child and that I was the one who had pursued being a foster parent. It had taken us several weeks to get a license, and he would not let me forget that it was my idea. I wanted to tell him to shut up. I said nicely in my sarcastic voice, "You did not stop me either. If we were pregnant, maybe we would not be going through this." That was not true, because long before it all, we both had a passion to help children. I was just angry. He had not been putting up with tantrums for more than a year and a half. He did not have to curb obsessive eating habits. He did not have to clean up urine, feces, and mucus. At that time, I felt like he was getting off easy, and I was screaming inside for someone to understand me and comfort me. Of course I could not see at the time that if he had not been at work, I would not have been able to be at home as much.

I loved Mary, but I did not know if my love would be enough or if I would be emotionally capable of taking care of her through childhood, adolescence, and young adulthood. Many times I felt like a mess myself, and since she had come, I had learned things about myself that I had never known. I learned about my limitations, my willpower, my insecurities, my faults, and more. I thought I was likeable until I realized that I did not even like me under stress. Adoption! Was I out of my mind?

She Really Loves You

She really loves you. I will never forget those words. One of the social workers said to me, "Most of these kids find it difficult to love after they have been in so many homes, and most of the time the parents are trying to show them affection and they will not accept it. But Mary, she really loves you." A part of me knew how much Mary loved me—so much that when the social worker spoke those words, I could not respond to her statement or look at her. The words had pierced my heart, but I could not let my guard down for fear that it might not actually be true.

Why did this child love me when most of the time I was agitated with her behavior? There were times when I was very gentle and kind to her, but it was very short-lived because then she would want to consume my time and energy by behaving in a manner that was simply revolting. I literally felt her taking my energy when I held her. It was as if I was filling this empty hole in her heart every time I held her, but at times that was a bit much for me, so I had to let go. I'd put her in her bed, often singing her to sleep, and then I would go and do the needed things around the house, all the while hoping that one day it would be enough. Maybe just one day someone would fill me back up. There were days when I completely understood what it meant to say, "I can't give what I don't have."

In my mind, *love* was a word people used too lightly to express their emotions toward a situation or person who made them feel good, but if that person no longer made them feel good, love was out of the door. This had been my experience on too many occasions, especially in friendship. I had very few friends who stuck by me in the good and the bad. And for the ones that did we had lost contact and they had new lives. Most people want to experience the good parts of you and would much rather not deal with the parts that are incomplete or not up to par.

My husband was the only one besides God who knew the most about me and still stuck around. If I wanted anything, he made sure I got it. I was free to be myself around him. I had felt for some time that I could not be myself around some people because they wanted a "perfect" me who knew how to fix their problems but did not want to hear about mine. In the presence of my husband, I could wash my hair or not wash my hair. I could wake up looking like the wrath of God was upon me and he still returned home. Of course by the time he returned, I always tried to look good for him. I guess it's important to look desirable to your spouse at some point in marriage. I'll never forget the time I had just awakened and he looked at me and said, "You are beautiful!" That meant a lot because he truly saw me. Yes, I needed more hugs and affection, and at one point I probably would have literally died if it meant that all my pain would subside. I suppose I had work to do, and part of it was to learn to love the rejected of this world unconditionally and learn to be loved by less-than-perfect people, including myself. It's hard to love unconditionally when you don't love yourself unconditionally, and it's hard to accept that maybe someone does actually love you.

Therapy Continues for Me

Every week after walking into this office that smelled like mildew, I wondered if I was really getting help or wasting money. I rationalized that at least I was able to talk about my feelings. The psychiatrist did not seem to offer much advice. I just mostly rambled on about stuff that had happened to me. It usually had to do with my past. My past had caused me the most trouble. I had issues with my family too. I love my family and always will, but some things still baffle me to this day.

I remember one event around my twenty-second birthday when I was just opening up about being abused to my mother and she was talking about the person who had sexually molested me. I became very angry, and understandably so. All the discomfort and the anger came to the surface and I did not want to see anyone's face, including hers. In the deepest part of me, I felt that she had not protected me. There was another person who knew as well but did not protect me. Both of these people were mild and timid in personality and may have feared the repercussions; nevertheless, I had been a child with little protection.

After talking to my mom, my dad came up the stairs to talk to me. He tried to console me, not knowing what to say, and even said the wrong thing, but his intentions were good. He also told me how upset my mother was because of the way I looked at her, although at that moment I don't know what else she expected. She had not protected me, and I blamed her. I really blamed her.

For some reason, I never really blamed my father even though I always felt something was wrong. He had tried to comfort me. I did resent the fact that they both chose to interact with this person in spite of his actions toward me. But my father was a pastor, and he just seemed to love anyone in spite of themselves. I wished that he would love this guy a little less, because it felt like betrayal to me. And wouldn't you know it, three days later after the incident with my mom he was invited over to the house and I would not come downstairs. Oddly, he kept asking for me. I thought it was disgusting. Many of my family members insisted that he had changed and that he was not the same man. And in his defense, it had been said that someone had given him drugs as a teenager that had allegedly messed up his mind. There may have been some truth to that, but when he tried to poison our family by putting pills in our milk, it did not seem to matter. We moved to the South to start a new life, but it was not long before he followed us there and was torturing us in our new home. On one occasion, he stood on the stairs, refusing to let us by. He also threw a broom at my little sister and hit her in the head. My aunt was able to escape past him to go and get help, and I, a little fighter even then, managed to get past him too and follow my aunt as she ran up the street to call the police. They all thought he had lost his mind, but when he heard that the police were coming, he had enough sense to calm down. That was a scary day, and I tried my best to stay away from him after that, but I always feared he would lose it.

On the day that he visited my parents by invitation, it took me hours before I would show my face, and even then I could not look at him. I have never understood why my parents did not call and at least say that this would not be a good day to come. Maybe they did not understand how deeply the abuse was affecting my life. They almost seemed naive to the situation. I don't think that some people really understand how badly abuse affects people. I still don't question the love my parents have for me, but some things I may never understand. I do know one thing: my dad loves people unconditionally and my mom tries to do the same and maybe they had already forgiven him. I still had a ways to go before my heart would not fear and resent him. I guess I was looking for true change and I did not trust him. Because of him there were few people whom I trusted or wanted to trust. I don't think I ever hated him, but I did not love him, either, and I sure would not leave my son or daughter alone with him. I had been a trusting child, but after he finished with me, those days were long gone. Therapy brought up all these issues for me and there were many times when I would sit with a nervous stomach before speaking, but I spoke in spite of myself to the man in the therapist's seat who had very little to say.

The Job

Years before my daughter arrived, I had starting working for a children's hospital as a nursing assistant and then as a medical assistant while pursuing a bachelor's degree in nursing. The very early years at the hospital were overwhelming. It was the very first time I had witnessed children being so sick. The illnesses ranged from respiratory illnesses to cancer. All of the children I helped to take care of were special, but the children with cancer and heart problems bothered my spirit the most. Most children with less severe illnesses usually got better after a few weeks, but the children with terminal illnesses often did not get better, and every time a child died, I felt my spirit get a little weaker and distraught. In spite of this, there was a part of me that loved the job and the interaction with the children. Most of all, I loved to hold the babies on the 3–11 shift. I would sing them to sleep to comfort them, but their little warm bodies falling to sleep on me comforted me beyond measure. It was the death of a child that bothered me so. One week three children passed way. Shortly after that another four-year-old passed away. I had prayed so hard for that child and really believed that God would intervene, but it did not happen as I thought it should. I had had faith in God from the time I was a child, in spite of people, and I was angry with him for not saving this child's life. After that I began to close up inside. It did not take much after that to discourage me. I remember one night after running around from patient to patient without taking a break or eating, a doctor took it upon himself to push my last button. Around 9:00 p.m. one of the nurses told me to take a break and I finally was able to sit down. Outside of the break room I heard the doctor asking, "Who has this patient? This baby needs to be changed." Now, I had just changed the baby an hour or so earlier, along with two other babies, and had fed them too, and I had only one feed left. In between patients I would come and comfort this particular baby because he was going through withdrawal from methadone. The mother of the child was on the drug while she was pregnant and had been a heroin addict before being put on methadone. The baby's meds were due, but I was not responsible for that and they had only been due at 9:00 p.m. Unfortunately, I guess Mr. Resident was on a rampage and dared not take it out on the nurse who had been a nurse for more than twenty-five years. She probably knew more than he did. Instead he embarrassed me. He called me out from the break room and proceeded to show me that this baby needed to be changed. You would have thought that he had discovered the cure for cancer, as loud as he was. I wanted to say to him, "Do you really think I know the exact moment a baby will poop? The baby could have pooped as soon as I went in for my break or maybe he pooped because you walked in the room. Or maybe he pooped because he was going through withdrawal and maybe, just maybe, he pooped for the simple fact that he just ate not too long ago and we humans have a tendency to do that." I knew that I took very good care of my patients, and that night it should have been enough to know that, but I was already hurting badly. The nurse quickly put him in his place and told me to finish eating and that she would take care of the patient. She also instructed the brilliant new doctor to turn off the lights in the patient's room that he had turned on, because too much light stimulation for a baby going through withdrawal was not good. He left, but he had already done his damage. Shortly after that I cut my hours to twenty a week and slowly dwindled away. The three days a week that I was there, I became consumed with the negative part of my job. There were missing limbs, cleft palate deformities, abused children, and more. After the cancer patients were moved to another floor, the pressure let up for a little while, but I just couldn't forget all that I had seen. I tried often to smile at work for the sake of my patients and their families and I did not stop caring for them, but I stopped praying. I was convinced that God did not care, so why should I pray to him? I was just a simple human with limited ability to change any situation, and although he was God, he just sat and watched. A part of me knew better than to accept that logic, but I had no more strength, and slowly depression crept in like a thief in the night.

After another year, I asked to go per diem. As time passed, I tried to put my effort into school and worked at the hospital only one or two days a week. I also picked up another part-time job working with children who had ADHD, ADD, were bipolar, and had various other mental disorders. I could not get away from children. I really loved them and I did well at this job, but the hospital was always in the back of my mind. The ironic thing is that the second job was preparing me to deal with my daughter's mental issues while she was being born right next door in the adjoining hospital, and at the time I had not a clue.

Some time passed, and issues surfaced at home. My husband was stressed from work and life, and so was I. I don't know why my husband and I never gave up on each other back then—we just didn't. Even when he was a young man getting into trouble when I first met him, I knew he would be my husband. We just stuck it out. I guess that is all you can do when you promise to be there in the good times and bad. And the fact that we both love each other dearly helped us not to give up. There was just always so much going on in my life. I was happy to be in school because I never thought I would get the opportunity to go back to college, but chemistry and advanced algebra were challenging, and working while taking care of my family proved to be quite a challenge. But the fact of the matter is, if my husband had not worked so hard, I would not have been able to work part-time and go to school.

My Mom

Years later, I was able to talk to my mom and straighten out some issues. I fell back in love with my mommy just because of a few words that she said. The words were, "Of course I was mad when I found out what was done to you. You were my little girl, and I loved you." There was something in those words that let me know that she really cared about what had happened to me. Initially, she had no idea what was occurring. After that my heart slowly began to mend. I did not resent her anymore, and I felt that she really did love me but had a very difficult time showing it. I felt that maybe she had been a victim as well, because back then, many people feared that man. He was pretty scary, and I remembered that once when I was little, he had thrown a brick at my mom's head and missed it by inches.

I began to think of the times when my mother would sew and how proud I would be as I watched her. Unfortunately, my mother was not very affectionate with me when I was a child, and I am not sure if she knew how much I wanted to be close to her. She would braid her hair in two pigtails, and I remembered thinking that I wanted to have thick, pretty hair like her. I did get the thick part. Those were the days before sickness struck her body.

In her mid-thirties my mom became very sick with lupus, and the medication she was given to treat it ruined her kidneys. She had already nearly died when she had my baby sister. Many days we were left without her, and when she was home, she was sick. She spent years on dialysis. My poor mom lost all of her beautiful hair and gained a tremendous amount of weight when she first got the diagnosis. Later, as the years passed, she was put on hemo-dialysis and taken off of prednisone. She lost an extreme amount of weight and looked frail, but she rarely complained. From time to time, she would end up in the hospital. Some part of me became used to her being sick all the time, but another part of me was tired for her and for our family. Why did she always have to be sick? Why couldn't we have a healthy mom?

My mom remained on dialysis for years until one night she received a call that would change her life and ours. She was getting a kidney transplant. As time passed, we began to see the mom we thought we had lost. She was vibrant and healthy looking, and her youthfulness appeared to return. I was glad to have her back in more ways than one.

The Accident

I was twenty-one and had just been married. My mom was sick and could not be at the wedding. One morning I was riding in the car to drop my husband off at work so that I could use the car later for work. My husband was in a rush because he was a little late. I told both him and my son to put on their seat belts. I heard my son putting on his seat belt, but my husband was very stubborn and always had to take longer just to prove that I was not telling him what to do. According to him, he was the boss man. Men! Anyway, no more than two minutes later, a car turning in from the opposite lane hit us. The man in the other vehicle did not have his lights on. The impact forced my husband's head against the window. Then his foot pressed against the gas pedal, causing the car to accelerate. We proceeded to cross into the opposite lane right into a telephone pole. I saw it happening and was in a daze. I could not turn the wheel. Everything seemed like a blur. I wanted to scream but could not, and so it just happened. The impact sent my head up against the dashboard, or so I think. It hit something. The seat belt locked on my stomach but for some reason did not lock across my chest. My husband's head lay on the seat without moving, and his eyes appeared glazed over making me think he was dead. I screamed at the top of my lungs to the only being I could remember who had helped me throughout my life. I began to scream, "Jesus! Jesus! Jesus! Please help!" Within moments I felt this warm presence on my right shoulder, and I calmed down. I was able to call 911 on my cell phone; back then cell phones actually looked like cordless home phones but it got the job done. I could see that my husband was starting to have seizures, and my son, looking bright eyed, was crying and saying, "Papa, don't die!" By this time a crowd had gathered and was watching. It always amazes me how people will stand and watch but take so long to go and get help. After a while I saw a few people running across the street, and I was able to tell a lady I had called the ambulance. My husband was seizing from time to time and to me that was comforting, because I knew at least he was alive. I tried to comfort him, but I could tell he was not responding to my words. At times he would get hysterical and begin to call for his mom. When the police and ambulance arrived, I was relieved. The medical technicians had to tie my husband down to keep him still and a woman cop kept saying, "If he'd just stop acting crazy, they could help him." Annoyed at her insensitivity, I responded, "He must have some kind of brain damage or he would not be acting that way, and for the record, that is my husband you are talking about." Later in the hospital, I found out just why he was acting that way. He had suffered brain damage, and for months after that, he did not remember our wedding and other memories. He knew I was his wife; he just did not remember how we came to that point. As time passed, memories would resurface and he would blurt things out about the past. He also suffered broken ribs, which took almost a year to heal. In addition, he had a fractured arm. I suffered trauma to my head with hemorrhaging in my left eye, a concussion, and other physical trauma. My son had a bruised eye. So for quite some time we were in pain and out of work. Therapy continued for about a year, and since the man who hit us did not have insurance, we had to look to our own insurance for help. Our car was totaled, we lost our apartment, and I lost my job, but we were alive. Eventually, we recovered money for our medical bills, which were extensive, but we were able to put some money aside for a home after living with my parents for eight months. Fortunately, we were young, so over time, our bodies healed. It's never easy going back to Mom and Dad after being out of the house for so long. Nevertheless, we did it. We survived, and so did they.

They Just Don't Know

Early on, I had been resentful of people who were loving toward my daughter, because I felt I had to do all the hard work and at the end of the day I had no more to give. They did not have to do anything for her, including dealing with her disturbing behavior. I just wanted to be away from everyone so that I could try to bond with her, but there were days that it was next to impossible. I remember days of pure exhaustion. I could barely get out of bed, and yet I had to help her get dressed, fix lunch, comb her hair, and make sure she was fed. Even when my husband helped with breakfast, it never seemed like enough. Under normal circumstances these responsibilities would not have vexed me so—it would have been my pleasure—but the pain in my life was so deep, I wanted to die. This child was taking more from me than I had to give, and my past was eating at me like cancer. Every day, for at least a year suicide was on my mind. I would think of ways to do it. Maybe I could take an overdose of sleeping pills. Maybe I could buy a gun and shoot myself, or maybe I could slice my arms. And one dark night, I sat in the bathroom sobbing with a razor blade in my hands. I began to make indentations on my forearm, and every time, I would press a little bit harder, hoping to feel something. I remember making six vertical lines and six horizontal lines, and as I began to start the last set of lines, my sobbing became uncontrollable because I knew that 666 was known to be the devil's number. I prayed for God to help me through the night and

85

let me feel just an ounce of love and I put the blade down to wash my arm. I had only broken the skin a little. By morning I figured it wouldn't be that noticeable. I went to bed with my eyes soaked from tears and my heart broken in so many places that I thought it would literally break. I cried myself to sleep and begged God to love me. The next morning I awoke by the grace of God with swollen eyes and only slight indications on my skin that something had gone wrong.

I felt alone for so long. I did not go to the church folk because I figured they'd tell me I should know better than to act that way and if I did find someone to understand, I would be too ashamed to share that kind of pain, so I kept it to myself. To this day, even as I share this, only God knows how deep the pain was. And it was so deep that at one point I decided to take my life and wrote this letter to my family:

To my family,

I am sorry for what I have done. I could not take it anymore. The sexual abuse I experienced as a child ate me alive. I don't want to be here anymore. I hope that God will have mercy on my soul, and I have asked him to forgive me. I asked him many times to help me, but it never lasted long. I'd feel better for a little while and then I would feel worse afterward. I just cannot do it anymore. I am a mess, and I would have never been better. I am so tired that I can't live. I cannot fight anymore.

My son, I love you. Please forgive me! My daughter, I love you. You will always be Mommy's girl. My husband, live! Don't let this stop you from doing the right thing. Live! Live! Live! I love you.

To my mom, dad, and sisters, I love you very much and I am sorry. I was a terrible mess inside, a broken spirit.

My best friend, I will always love you. I am sorry with all my heart.

To all of the friends and family at church, I tried and I tried but it overtook me. But don't you give up. I was broken inside.

And in very large letters I wrote,

My body aches! My spirit is gone! I am tired!

I know it had to be God that pulled me through another night of near death. Until my daughter came, I did not know this type of pain existed in my life. I spent many years dressing and playing the part of a perfect woman. I could do a perfect hairstyle. I could dress myself like a glamour queen and apply makeup to look fabulous, yet I did not know the deepest part of myself. I was a lost child within, and every day I looked at my daughter, she reminded me just how lost I was. In many ways I was her. She screamed from her abuse. I screamed inside. She threw tantrums when she did not know what to do with her emotions, and I yelled and screamed. She had bad dreams about her past and was cranky if anyone touched her in her sleep. I was the same way. Every day I looked at her, I was forced to ask myself if I could love myself. The ironic thing is that she came to me at around the same age I was when I was abused. We shared many things, yet I wanted to run from her and love that part of her all at the same time. Impossible to do, I felt, because that meant I would have to accept that part of me. This battle was inside of me, and I was so afraid that the ugly part would win and that I would die. I would die eventually, but only to the spiritually broken and wounded part of me that needed to die so that I could really live. But it took some time, and boy did I feel some suffering in the meantime. I wanted everyone away from me and I think some people felt it, because many seemed to stay away after a while, and it was better that they did. I didn't have enough to give anyone else. I barely had enough for my family, and depression wants room for no one but itself and was trying its best to take over. One night when I was severely depressed I wrote this poem:

Nobody Loves Me

Nobody loves me,
and it seems few people care.
My mind is really tired and
life just doesn't seem fair.

I live in a world where people expect you to be
nice all the time,
and the Lord has you as this perfect,
pleasant doll.

It's all baloney—nobody is that happy all the time;
even with God, life is hard.
Frankly, if I did not think that I would go to hell,
I would kill myself.

I don't believe that people are really truthful about what they feel.
Half of us are barely surviving but want to act as if it's "all good."

It's not all good.
It's not as it should be.
It's not all peaches and cream.
It's actually dreadful.

And sometimes waking to the morning is a task.
You don't need to ask why,
'cause if you were honest,
You'd probably say the same.

Nobody loves me, and I know it, and who can blame them?
I need too much.
I need affection in the worst way.
I need hugs.
I tried to get love, but they all leave, and who can blame them?
I suck.
I am nobody.

Going through a life crisis,

I even hate myself.
I am useless.
I am nothing.

I try, but why?
I need love, but I'd rather die.
Nobody loves me,
and like I said, who can blame them?

I hurt the people I love,
and when they don't love me,
I hurt them more.
And I will keep doing it
because it's who I am.

I've crept out on men who don't love me
and then gone to someone who will never love me.
I try to love the Lord with all my heart, but I don't even love myself.

My womb is empty.
My heart is cold.
Nobody loves me, and I am alone.

No hugs,
No love,
No kisses,
Just because.

Go to your side of the bed.
This side is mine.
Stay on your side of the circle.
Give me my pillow now.

And if I happen to grab the wrong one,
it is snatched from under my head
as if I am not there,
And the pillow is more important than me trying to rest.

In rest, I pretend I am not here anyway,
and when I am awakened harshly,
I know that I am still here

and nobody loves me.

Nobody loves me.
Nobody loves me.
Why live?
Why try?
Just die.

It will never be as I dreamed or wished.
Nobody loves me, and I know it.
Why live?
Why try?
Just die.

Well, of course it was not true that I was not loved. And it surely was not true that my husband did not love me. One of the reasons he agreed to adopt in the first place was that I wanted to. My perceptions were real to me, though, and I felt in my mind that somehow it had to be true that I was not loved. I needed someone to be gentle with me, but admittedly I was like a rosebush, thorny on the outside and soft on the inside, and it's hard to get close to a rosebush in spite of its beauty. And sometimes people just don't know how to love gently when they are broken themselves.

I'll Never Leave You

I have heard the phrase *I will never leave you* several times, but it was never honored. They left and it was abrupt. It was always from people I deeply loved. Sometimes I think my heart still suffers from this anguish. I used to think my heart had been broken in places impossible to mend. I felt God's touch in my heart. I felt him heal parts of me that were broken, but every time he did, there was a bomb waiting around the corner to rupture me. Whether through friendships or through a loss, I felt I did not have time to exhale before my breath was taken from me. I did not trust anyone, including myself, during these times, because I knew that when I was in pain, I was quite capable of using my tongue to cut metal in half. It wasn't by cursing or using vulgar language but by simply disregarding the emotional effect my harshness would have on a gentle soul. Just as people had shut me out, I knew how to do it to others. I was good at it because it was all I knew how to do when I was in pain. It felt like it was protection against a cold world. I felt I had to be cold to endure the coldness of others. The problem was that it did not sit well with my soul. When I was mean, I literally felt sick. When I was cold with my words, I felt emotionally protected but sick. I knew it was not who I wanted to be, but then, it was all I felt I needed to be. I needed to survive.

I remember the first man who ever broke my heart. You'd think it would be the man who molested me because he stole my innocence, my childhood, my trust in adults, my peace, and so many other things, but it was not him; it was my dad. After I was traumatized, I was expected to not speak of it. I started to get more spankings and he appeared to be colder toward me. I did not understand how a man who had loved me so much a few years before could become so serious and treat me as if I were a little adult. I was expected to do everything perfectly. It was tiring. My life felt tiring. I remember playing very little, and the times that I did are embedded in my mind because I was so happy when I could just be free. Those moments did not last long.

And my dad, well, I felt like he left me and instead of feeling loved, I felt sad. I registered the rejection in my mind and figured that if my dad could leave me, then anyone could, and they did. Leaving someone is not always physical. The inability to make time for them, hug them, comfort them, and enjoy their presence can be just as bad. Sometimes it is worse because they see you but cannot have the parts of you that they desperately need. I missed him and our relationship. I really loved my daddy, but then he became my judge and I did not like him.

Anger

Ever think you could really bite a nail and the nail would break in half but your teeth would remain intact? I felt that way on a couple of occasions and had trouble figuring out why I felt that way. There is a verse in the Holy Bible that reads, "Be ye angry and sin not" (Ephesians 4:26 KJV). I was angry and sinning. Oftentimes, I had valid reasons for being angry, but having to get people back for hurting me was wrong. Sometimes there was no real thought-out process behind it; I just ignored them or did not give them the time of day. It was important to me to share with them my resentment for their actions. So much for "Vengeance is mine; I will repay, saith the Lord" (Romans 12:19 KJV). There were days when I thought of some people in the church as my enemy. I could not stand to look at some of them. I did not want to go to church anymore. In my heart I loved God, but his Word says that I can't love him and hate my brother so I stopped talking to God again. Big mistake, because I needed him like I needed air, and even in my sadness, depression, anger, bitterness, resentment, and hurt I believed that he knew I wanted badly to please him. Sadly, though, I was lost—lost in pain and angry at the world. Suicide was looking better by the moment.

My heart's desire was to keep trying to help my daughter, to see the progress in her life instead of the failures, to love my husband without reservation or fear, to be so connected to God that it did not matter whether there was war to contend with or the sun was shining like on a beautiful summer day. Trusting God means that everything does not have to be perfect in order to be happy, but I was not there yet and was convinced that maybe I never could be.

At that time the only person in my life I seemed to love deeply and unconditionally was my son. Even during his teenage years when he was cruel to me and barely spoke to me, I loved him through it. From his birth, he was a pleasant child. He could do no wrong in my eyes, even when he probably deserved to be in trouble. I loved to take him with me everywhere I went and wanted to be in his presence. He often made me smile when he was young, and nothing much seemed to bother him. He had a quiet demeanor and very rarely cried. So imagine my surprise when I learned that I had just been blessed with a pleasant child when I had my son and that not all children were this way.

It Never Lasts Long Enough

When I would start to feel better about the situation and myself, it never lasted for long. In years past, there were maybe a few times that I was the person I wanted to be. Inside my heart, I was a tender soul wanting to love unconditionally, but outwardly the shell in which I hid protected me from being hurt, and that is what those close to me saw. They are the ones who could have hurt me the most. It was easier to accept those who could not cause me a world of hurt or were easier to deal with. They were less dangerous. My daughter, on the other hand, was wild, hyperactive, and out of control and would someday have the ability to cause more harm to me by finding her biological family after all the emotional sacrifices that had been made. My mind was not clear, and I was damaged. I was selfishly consumed in depression and pain.

What If I Just? ...

What if I just did everything that I felt? I felt like slapping a few people around sometimes. When my husband made me mad, I felt urges to hit him in the head with a frying pan. When my dogs barked excessively and urinated in my house, I felt like picking them up and throwing them out. When my daughter threw tantrums, I felt like shaking her till she stopped. When my son ignored me after I had called him a million times, I wanted to throw something. What if I followed through on it all? What if one night when I was tired of being depressed, I just took my life and did not care about the consequences? What if I punched the people at church in the face who were so busy judging everybody else that they could not see themselves? I knew I was messed up, but did they know that some of them were too? I was critiquing myself enough; I did not need them judging me too. What if I just threw in the towel and said enough of people, enough of me, enough of my family, and I will sin like the worst sinner and not look back? What if I had followed through on all my thoughts? The truth is I would probably be dead or dying, in jail or going to jail, alive but not living. You see, the mind will have you do many things that are not right and tell you to excuse your indiscretions. And once the acts are committed, they cannot be taken back. The love I have for my family is undeniably deep, so to hurt them would have damaged my soul. The people at church were just people with their own faults looking to be saved by grace. Emotions will cause you to act before you think, so it's important for them to be in check. If you are used to reacting to everything you feel, your emotions are in control, not you. Remember, dwelling in the past is just like eating digested food over and over again. No one wants to do that because it would be disgusting. So why continue to do that to your mind? I really struggled in this area and parts of me did not want to let go of the past, because in many ways it gave me ammunition to fight back when I was wounded. Sick? Maybe, but the only way to heal is to be real.

Weight Gain

When I first met my husband, I was five feet four inches tall, but for years thought I was an inch taller than that. Many of us enjoy thinking we are an inch taller. I was also 115 pounds. Over about twelve years I had put on about twenty-five pounds, which I guess is normal, but in the years that I struggled with depression I was putting on a few pounds every month. I remember getting on the scale in November and then being weighed again in the spring and I had put on twelve pounds. I remember thinking, How in the world did that happen? I was thicker around the waist by almost three inches and my size 6 was now a size 9 and breaking into the world of size 10. Now, for some people reading this, the thought of going from a size 6 to a 9 may not a big deal, but I had done it in less than five months. I went to the doctor to find out if I had a thyroid problem, but the test results were negative. I continued to go to several specialists because I was not feeling like myself. I was frequently tired and irritable, and constantly felt bloated. I went to three specialists. One suggested that I give up my foster daughter because he thought I was depressed. The others did not say this but prescribed me Cymbalta and Celexa, which are both medications for depression. *My goodness*, I thought, *do I sound and look that depressed?* So I tried to go to the gym to work out, and although it did make me feel better, getting there was a bigger issue. I had so many stresses in my life that I just wallowed in it till I could not wallow anymore. I did what I had to do with no enthusiasm and only to get by. I was not living a fulfilled life but only surviving, and soon my body began to break down. I became truly sick with back pain, stomach pain, muscle aches, joint pain, nausea, and other symptoms.

I was not happy with myself during this time, and I was consumed with fear.

The Lump

One night before going to bed I felt a lump in my left breast. I was instantly encompassed with fear because I knew how I had been feeling. I made an appointment to see my doctor, who confirmed that it was indeed a lump. Shortly afterward, an ultrasound was done of my breast. For days I was worried. Days turned into what seemed like weeks, and then I had to decide if I wanted it surgically removed or aspirated. I chose aspiration, and that day I was thankful that my husband was with me, because I had been alone in many scary moments of my life. As time passed, I made peace with the fact that I might be sick. I pictured my hair falling out and having my head wrapped in a scarf. I wondered how I would look with no hair. I hated my forehead because I thought it was too round, and it had a small scar from a fight as a teenager, but then I thought, who would care? I also pictured walking beside my husband looking sick as other people stared at me. I prepared myself for the fact that I might die, and I thought at least I would be out of the misery of this world and would be with God. Now, all of this was before the results came back. A week later, I found out that the lump was not cancerous. I was relieved but oddly disappointed that I would have to continue to live. I did still thank God for life because I knew many women had not received the same results I had. I also knew that life was precious; I just did not feel like a precious asset to it.

During this time I never breathed a word to my family or

friends about the lump because I did not want to talk about it, nor did I want to share something so personal. I did not want people looking at my breast in a strange manner and giving me the sympathetic look. Later, I told a few people, but that was it and I let it be.

My Sisters

I am the oldest of seven girls, and they are all beautiful. One of the blessings of our home growing up was the gift of seven girls, each of whom is unique in her own way. The first sister is very abrupt in her speech and tries to act as if things don't really affect her, but she has a heart to help others and give. She does not even blink when it's time to give up something; she just does it. She is also funny in her expressions and will have a meaningful conversation with me on the phone but will not say good-bye. All of a sudden I'll just hear a click. She needs the gentleness of a kind-hearted person in the worst way. The second sister is sweet and soft-spoken and doesn't say a lot, but she too needs the deep understanding of a person who will not reject her. At times she can be sarcastic and you either start laughing or think, *What did she mean by that?* The third sister is funny, funny, and funny. She does things that no one else can get away with. She needs affection but does not know how to react to it. She too is kind and generous, and she is a wonderful mother. My fourth sister is very creative, sweet, has a giving nature and is often taken advantage of because her nature is passive. She deserves better than what she has accepted in the past, but I believe the right person will show up one day. My fifth sister is not passive by nature but also can be very loving. She is a wonderful mother of three beautiful boys. She is also helpful to others. I think all of us have feared rejection at some point and have in the past tended to be people-pleasers. Last but not least is my baby sister. She does not talk a lot, but she is wise. At times, though, she is solemn and seems ahead of her years. She was not suppose to live through birth and yet here she is, and wonderfully made. They all have a special place in my heart and always will. Sometimes we do not have to speak; we just know the unspoken. And from us have come grandchildren that my parents are blessed to enjoy. I pray that one day all of us will be made well in body, mind, and spirit.

True Beauty

What is true beauty? Am I beautiful? Will someone see me as beautiful when I am old? Or will they pass me by and say, "Look at that old lady"? My heart was full of all these kinds of things that I'd like to do, but many times fear stopped my progress: fear of not being accepted, fear of someone not seeing me for me, or fear of being seen for me and then rejected. Years ago I said a prayer that God would release me from my fears, and he did, from many of them. We have to be willing to let go and let God. Shortly after that time I wrote a poem that expressed the desperate need that many of us have to be accepted.

Why am I Afraid to be Me

Why am I afraid to be me?
I'm five feet four and like to say I'm five five.
It's in my mind:
I'm not tall enough,
strong enough,
good enough for society.

I'm five feet three,
skinny and smart,
but my nose is too big.
My teeth are too wide apart.
My hair is not long enough.

People don't look at me because I'm pretty;
they look at me because I'm weird.
I appear to be strange, out of range,
afraid I'm not good enough.
No, I'm just not good enough.

I'm five feet eight.
I'm the perfect weight.
But I don't like myself.
Who am I anyway?
Am I becoming what people want?
Or who I want to be?
So much pressure.
Can I be me?

I'm five feet two.
I don't look like you.
You're so pretty; I'm not.
Your eyes are beautiful.
Mine are not.
I look like an ordinary person.
You have a stride in your walk.
Why can't I be like you?
I do not like who I am,
so I'll keep my head down,
with a frown.

Why should I look up?
No one will notice me anyway.

I'm five feet nine.
Nice height, right?
But why do I have to be white?

All these ethnic people,
their hair is always in a different style.
My hair is always the same.
It's been this way for a while.
They look so different.
I am so plain.

I am five feet.
Why can't I be tall and look like a model?
I am not pretty enough.
My skin is too dark.
Why can't I be lighter or whiter?
I am simply just not enough.

I'm six feet tall,
and I am a model.
Everyone is always glaring and staring,
but they never see my heart.
I am a person underneath,
though they can't seem to see.
I'm afraid that when I age,
I will be completely forgotten.
I want to be loved,
but they can't see past my body.

I'm five feet one inch,
if I am lucky.
I'm big and round.
The car moves when I get in.
Do you think anyone will notice?
Do you think they will see?
Why do I have to be big and ugly?

I could deal with just one.
My sister told me that I look nice today.
I don't believe her.

She just said that to try to make me feel good.

Afraid to be me,
Afraid to be me.
Who are we not to be free of this slave mentality?
The chains could come off,
but we keep them on.

With our claim for fame to be
the perfect face,
the perfect body,
the perfect spouse
with the perfect job,
to have the perfect house
in the perfect neighborhood.
To go to the perfect church,
to be the perfect pastor,
the perfect first lady,
the perfect usher,
the perfect deacon,
the perfect choir director,
the perfect teacher,
the perfect, the perfect, the perfect—
no such thing, I'm afraid

And as I continued to write this poem this answer entered my spirit:
take off the reins, my people.

Take off the expectations
and praise my name.
Bondage, bondage, bondage—
my people should be free.
Look to me;
you're beautiful to me,
even when the world may not see.

All of this tragedy—affliction, oppression, want for possessions,
drug addictions, alcoholism, broken homes, messed-up lives,
divorce, abuse, and neglect—
so much to work on,
so much to work on.
Your body will fade away,
and what will you have done by the end of your life to please me?
When you were so busy
trying to make it all right,
afraid and wasting time,
so much time.
Break free, my people.
Break free and praise me!

It was easier for me to express my feelings through words, and
when my spirit was open to it, I could continually write without
fear. Often it felt as if the answers came right from heaven. The
problem was that many times I was not open to it because I
thought I could figure it out myself. I thought God's answers were
often simple but hard to apply to my life. I thought to myself,
*Sounds good but I cannot praise God and follow his way when
sometimes I want to die.*

Finding the Will to Live

It's quite a sad thing to say that as a Christian, I often did not want to live. I wanted God to take me out of here in the worst way, but I knew that committing suicide was probably not the best way to try to get to heaven. I remember one night having a dream about stabbing someone. It was then that I knew that there were evil forces working in my life to cause me to harm someone else or better yet myself. When I slept, it felt natural, but when I awoke, I felt sick, disgusted, and in utter disbelief that I could dream such a thing. The rage in my dream was unbelievable. The control was sickening, but it felt so needed. There were many days that I awoke feeling as if the life had been taken from me during the night. But during that time, I had chosen to stop talking to God because I was angry with him, and a part of me wanted to do things my way. I knew God's presence could not be a part of anger and rage. I did not stop believing in God, nor did I tell him that I no longer wanted his presence in my life. I just stopped communication, and the further I was away from his presence, the easier it was for evil to get closer. As a little girl, I was tortured in my sleep; I would wake up with scratches all over me. I would dream of animals coming to get me and would awake, petrified of the dark. It did not help that the person who abused me had also attacked me one night in my sleep by hitting me in the leg with a blunt object. I thought I had been shot, and he had run out of the house. Those were some crazy days back then, and I had felt helpless. As I was older, I would picture walking to his house to ask him why he had hurt me. Before he could answer, I'd shoot him and feel better. There were parts of me that wanted to get him out of my mind and soul and not give him the power to control my life. The other part wanted to get him back. I think I had mixed emotions and did not know what to do with them. Every time I thought I was over it, it returned like a nightmare on a clear evening. I had poor self-esteem and continued to cover it behind a tough exterior. This up-and-down behavior continued until I decided I was too tired of being on a roller coaster. I told myself that I had to fight even if it took years to overcome this depression. It would be a little bit at a time, but I had to do it. I knew I could not find the will to live without God, so I prayed for his mercy, asked for his forgiveness, and asked him to help me forgive. And the journey began ...

First I started to wake up in the morning with a more pleasant attitude even if it hurt me. It took about two months to change my way of thinking in the morning. Slowly, I started to feel normal in the morning. There were days that I felt cranky, but I pushed past the feelings. Whenever a negative thought entered my mind, I would not entertain it; I would quote a Bible verse or replace it with a good thought. I would often say, "This is the day the Lord has made; let us rejoice and be glad in it." Before that time, I could not stand people who awoke in the morning singing or happy. The next step was learning how to deal with my daughter's bizarre, strange, and oppositional behavior. I prayed to God for help with this as well. I knew that I was not capable of doing it alone. First, I had to accept that she was truly mine, because for so long I had been reminded that she was not biologically mine. I also thought that I would spend years taking care of her and then one day she would want to find her biological mom anyway. As I processed this, the thought came to me that her biological mother was not truly a mom. A mom sticks with you through thick and thin, feeds you, clothes you, tries to protect you from a harsh world, listens to you call her a thousand times and still answers, packs lunches, washes clothes, sings to you, reads you stories, corrects you when you're wrong, and most important, loves you unconditionally. I decided to accept her as indeed mine and that if the time came that she wanted to find her biological mom, I would pray again for strength to help her, because that is what unconditional love does. When she acted out, I'd pray instead of speak, and give myself time to think clearly first. I knew that mentally she had been affected by her abusive history so I had to accept that she might not ever be what I wanted her to be. Ideally, she would learn to find her way since she was being guided by love. I forgave her for the things she had done to bring stress into my life. I never looked at myself again as a long-term babysitter but as a mom and a special one at that, because I was trusted to take care of a child who was not born to me but who had entered my heart in the midst of complete chaos. I wrote my daughter a poem to express my feelings about her. It read like this:

Dear Mary, My Daughter,

I cried for you, and you came to me.
I looked for you, and there you appeared.
You were in my heart long before you came,
and since you came into my life. it has not
been the same.
We struggled together to find our way and
now you're in my heart to stay,
birthed in my heart,
though you did not grow in my belly.
It is you that I see as my little Mary.
From the arms of many you left
to find the comfort of my arms,
and as long as I live with God's help,
I will not abandon you
and make you cry.
I will not give you away
and tell you another lie.
It is with God's love that I will be diligent
in your upbringing.
It is with his love
that I will teach you right from wrong.
I will not be perfect,
but I will love you, child,
your smile, your heart, and every inch of you.
Love,
Mommy
To God be the glory for all he did to restore in me the will to live
and to love.

Forgive My Husband Too?

Oh no! I thought. *Not him too.* I met my husband several years ago, just before I was about to turn eighteen. By that time, I already had a five-month-old child. I loved my son, and he filled my life with joy. He meant the world to me after losing my first baby. Sometimes I can't believe I had these experiences when I was still a child myself. It's amazing to me now that I survived and am still here with my right mind. However, I was not ready to be a mom but had to figure it out.

Guided by attraction and drawn by chemistry, I met my husband one day as I saw him riding down the street on a motorcycle. He stopped, we talked, and after a few dates, the rest was history. He was eye-catching and there was something about him I really liked, though when we first met, he was mentally lost in the streets. In spite of this, he was gentle with my child, and I saw very early on that he loved him. Regarding other things, though, I was naïve, and I was often filled with apprehension and joy when I saw him. Sometimes I did not know what to expect. At times he was very kind. In anger, he was physically aggressive toward me, but I had no problem fighting him back, and I am not sure he was used to that. At times, he would say something hurtful and I would swing first. As I think of it now, more than twenty years later, it almost seems as if it did not happen because things are so much more peaceful. We are in love beyond what we ever imagined. I cannot imagine something like that happening now. He is my best friend, and I love him dearly. And as I said before, he knows more about me than any other person and really sees me and accepts me. But it took years to get here. We have suffered through addiction, affliction, anger, anxiety, and the absence of true love until we stopped fighting each other and joined forces for our relationship to work. However, I had to forgive him first for every time he hurt me and for years of mistrust brought on by his desire to use drugs and do other things that were harmful to him and our relationship. For a while I gave up and joined him until I realized that no amount of alcohol or drugs could soothe the pain that had been stored inside my soul. I chose to forgive him and let go of trying to change him, and that is when the change began to come. I had spent many nights literally sobbing because of his lifestyle and how it affected our lives. Then one night, I said to God, "I'll let him go and you can have him to do as you please." Of course God did not need my permission to work on someone, but he did need me to get out of the way, because I worshipped my husband more than I trusted God. And when I realized this, I wrote this poem:

Am I Trusting God or Man?

Why do I say that I am trusting God
when man is constantly on my mind?
Why do I say I love God
but man occupies my time?

Why do I say I don't feel God near?

But I am too busy shedding tears over man.
Why do I cry for the peace of God?
But I won't let it all just be.

Why do I try to fix the people that I say I love?
To make my world calm,
am I not supposed to be
in God's arms?

Why do I defend my behavior
as if it's okay to let them be my god?
Have I looked at the god I am serving lately?

It does not love me right
or hold me tight.
Its love is fleeting and speaks such harsh words.
It is not kind,
and I'm letting it drive me out of my mind.

What kind of god is this that couldn't care less about my heart?
And every opportunity it gets, it tears me apart.
What kind of god is this that should dare come between me
and the God who created heaven and earth?

This replacement god
does not even know how to embrace.
It seems more messed up than me,
yet I continually serve it

as if it will change by some will of my own.
I have trusted in this god for what only God can do,
and yet it seems to consume me with its ways.
It drives me a moment away from being insane.

Jesus never drove me crazy
and then pushed me to the side.
Jesus never told me he loved me

and then left me behind.

Why is this alternative god so important to me?
Do I feel that I am not worthy of having or being or existing?
This god did not wash away my sins
or give me a new way of life.

Yet I chase it.
I lose sleep over it.

I must find my way back to my God,
the holy one,
the awesome one,
the faithful one,

the way, the truth, the life.
Old mean god of the present,
I let you go
to be handled by the one
that can make
you bow.

The one that guided Moses
led Joshua,
anointed David,
guided Elijah,
and saved me.

I will no longer serve you
but hand you over to my God
as Moses did with Pharaoh,
as David did with Saul,
as Joseph did with his brothers.

I will serve my God,

my king.

I will humble myself before his mighty being,

remembering that he is my God,

not you, or you, or you.

My God beats all the gods of the world,

and so I shall follow him all the days of my life,

even though following him will cause the other gods to fight.

It's okay, because I already know that my God wins.

Whatever was I thinking to replace God with anyone or anything?

I must have been lost or sleeping, but now that I am found and awake,

I will forsake all for his namesake.

I slowly begin to breathe a sigh of relief on my way out the door. I began to look for apartments and was starting to put together a budget for my new single life that would include my daughter and my son. I did not care about the house, the cars, or my possessions. I desired peace.

One Sunday, I had decided to go into the prayer line at church, and as the pastor began to pray for me, he spoke one word: "Stay!" I thought to myself, *Oh c'mon, enough already, I'm ready to go.* I knew that it was from God because I had told no one of my plans. I was obedient, and by some miracle, I watched the man I had been married to for years turn into someone wonderful. I cannot say it enough: *God is amazing!*

The beauty of forgiving and healing is that you can start over without the baggage. Now he is almost the man I dreamed of. Men are always works in progress. Come on, laugh: it's funny how we women are always trying to change our men. They have to want it too or it will never happen, and God knows how to work on their hearts better than we do. Sometimes by trying to control things we can make them worse. I knew that the man I met that day on the motorcycle would play a huge part in my life, but I was not prepared for the ride. But once I let go, God equipped me.

I am excited to say that I now have a man who works diligently to provide for his family. He is a wonderful father and a good husband. I want for nothing, and anything I need that is in his power to give, I am given. I have love in my family. And when things come to try to disrupt that, I remind myself that "no weapon formed against me shall prosper" (Isaiah 54:17 KJV). We are blessed that things turned out this way; they often do not. I am again thankful for the power that abides in the name of Jesus. I do not desire to be swept away by another. I am content and happy with the man that I have, and I love my family even when things get tough. I have a son, a daughter, and two fluffy white dogs, and if God sees fit, he may even bring another child from this womb.

The Abuser Apologizes

I truly did not think this day would come, but it did, at a funeral. My grandmother passed away from cancer. I had many mixed emotions because I had always thought that she knew I was being abused and chose not to say anything. I don't really blame her, because I did not understand her life or the things she went through. I just did not know how to have a relationship with her. When she was on her deathbed, I spoke to her and told her I loved her while holding her hand. She smiled and then seemed to slip back into her drug-induced state. She was on morphine for the pain and did not live long after being admitted into a hospice facility. I was happy that I went to see her. She was my grandmother, and I hope to see her in heaven one day.

I dread funerals. They are so sad, and everyone is grieving. When I die, I want people to be happy that I am out of this world and that my destination is to spend eternity with Jesus. As people cried at the funeral, they also talked about her destination, which made it less gloomy; still I felt like I was in a daze. Good thing I was, because the inflictor of a lot of my pain asked to speak with me. For some odd reason I chose to let him. He held my hand and said, "I am sorry for any pain I caused you." I don't know why I allowed him to hold my hand. For the first time, it just did not feel creepy. I simply replied, "Thank you" and walked away. I needed to hear him say that, and even though I appreciated it, I went through a variety of emotions. At first, I could not believe it and was thankful that he recognized his wrong. Then I was angry that I had let him touch me. Later, I felt confused and did not know what I felt. Now I don't think I hate him, but I'm not sure I love him either. The blessing is that I don't hate him. I don't like to think of him, and as a matter of fact it took me a while to be able to write this chapter. I kept avoiding it because I did not want to go to dark places that messed up my mind. I know that for anyone who has suffered abuse, it was important for me to write about this. And it was healing for me as well. I have no desire to be controlled by my past. I have no desire to be controlled by the actions and thoughts of others. They are not my God, and surely my birth into this world was not meant for evil purposes, so I must live freely.

There are brief times where I almost feel sad for him. What made him commit such acts? What made him stoop so low as to touch a child? Was he insane or was he too disturbed to make the right choices? I don't know and I probably never will, but he is not the dictator of how my life will be, nor is my father, my mother, or any other person. We all make choices that can make our lives more difficult or easier to live. Sometimes we are harmed by someone else's choice, but God is not to be blamed for that; rather he is the healer. I hope that one day I will be able to tell this man that I have forgiven him, but even if that day never comes, I will not allow him to have any power over me. I wish him the best in his new life in Christ, but I have a life to live without fear, so I am moving along.

Forgive Myself

Oh, this was the hardest of all. I was so displeased with the things that I had done over my life. There were so many that I lost count. Maybe I was so stuck on doing everything right that I was doing many things wrong. I was taught very early in my life that doing things right meant you were good. The problem was that I could not keep up because I was so messed up. When I had bad thoughts about people or did "bad things," I would go over it in my head for a long period of time. I also struggled with a fiery temper, although it seemed to be under control until my daughter came along. Maybe she had come for the purpose of helping me deal with everything I had swept under the carpet. When she came, insecurity, hurt, and rejection were at the surface and some days I literally thought I would die. I was more uncomfortable than I had ever been with myself.

In my early twenties, I had returned to church, and in my late twenties, I was caught up in a world of chaos, trying to deal with my internal issues. I really did not know that I was so unstable or maybe the things that happened to me made me unstable. I did know that I felt extremely broken. Broken people can do some serious damage to others and themselves. I had much to forgive myself for, including being involved with people who were not good to me or for me. They were simply destructive. In my young years, I was around people who had no good intentions for me but I could not see it. I thought they needed me, and when they fed me lies or manipulated me, I thought they actually cared. Looking back now, I know I deserved better. It was a bit ridiculous, but my self-esteem was shot and I had not a clue. I thought I was in control, but I was completely wrong, because the result was pain. Some parts of my life are too painful to be explicit about them. The point is, I needed to forgive myself for bad choices and did not know how, so I hurt other people with my words.

There was a period when I chose not to say anything if it was not nice. I remember the day when I decided that I did not care anymore and would say whatever I wanted, when I wanted, because I was tired of being walked on. I wish I had not made that conscious choice, because it was difficult to shut my mouth after that. It was like a weapon.

When my daughter would act out, I would tell her to stop acting crazy and leave me alone. Or I would say, "Just go—you are getting on my last nerve." On some occasions I would just point to where I wanted her to go and say, "Move your behind or I'll move it for you." I'd give her looks that could kill. A few times I popped her on the mouth for being disrespectful, cursing, and giving me what I called unbelievable attitude. But they were just poor excuses for not finding a better way to discipline her. She was wrong, but I was not right. Some parents may find that kind of discipline acceptable for a smart-mouthed or difficult child, but it did not sit well with my spirit. Yes, there is a Scripture in regard to discipline that refers to sparing the rod and spoiling the child. He that spareth his rod: hateth his son, but he that loveth him chasteneth him be times (Proverbs 13:24 KJV). But I am sure that there is nothing that supports disciplining out of frustration and anger. In addition to that, she was repeating what she had learned from other places she had lived. It was what she knew. Afterward, I felt bad, which would lead to guilt and feeling worse. So clearly, it was not beneficial. I remember at the age of fifteen when I cursed at my father because he would not let me go out. He responded by smacking me on both of my cheeks so hard that I fell to the ground. There were imprints on my face from his hands for three days. I meant it when I spoke those words to him, because I was really angry with him for many things. My mom's friend took me in for a few days so that I could go to school and things could cool down. She introduced me to makeup so that I could cover up the marks, and after that, makeup became my friend for better or worse. Was my dad wrong? Yes, but so was I for the way in which I conveyed my message. At the time, I was just simply out of control.

Now, maybe all the things I said to my daughter were true, but did I really have to say them? Did I really have to pop her on the mouth? No. I think there were better ways to deal with it, but I was fed up with her and myself. There was no arguing that she was a difficult child, but when she first came to us, I had more patience with her and things had been ten times worse. But after a while, I had had enough, so by the time she was better, I had very little tolerance for any defiance. In my mind, I had put up with enough from everyone, including her. However, there was no excuse. I was still wrong.

Years later, my dad came to me and asked me to forgive him for anything he had done to hurt me. It was the right timing, because as soon as he asked, the desire was already there to forgive him and to start a new relationship. I love my dad. In spite of his errors, he is the best father he knows how to be to all of his girls.

My daughter did not ask to be hurt by her abusers, and God knows it was not my desire to hurt her even a little bit. I love my family, so I had to forgive everyone, including myself. It was difficult, and though some say it is simple to forgive, I had to work hard at it.

The Fast

My dad is the pastor of the church to which I belong. He asked all the members to fast for an entire month. He requested this every February. Now, every year until this point I had tried, but I had never quite succeeded at lasting the entire month. Quite honestly, I thought he was out of his mind for requesting such a thing. Inside I said, *That's easy for you to do; you're a pastor and you are used to it.* Even so, I committed to doing it because I had been praying for God to change things in my life; although some things were better, there were some other things that I was not pleased with. I also wanted change for others. And the Bible clearly states the importance of fasting and prayer. The four main requests that I had prayed for were to be free of hurt, lack of forgiveness, anxiety, and fear. They are all connected. First I was hurt, then I chose not to forgive, and this produced anxiety, which resulted in fear. I had a fear of building relationships and of crowds, and most important, I was petrified to love. I had been hurt so much over the years that I was really just afraid to be kind, gentle, or loving. The love was there, but it was blocked because I had refused to be vulnerable again. Though my will to live and to love had returned, I did not let the action of love flow freely. I was in a troubled state, and I wanted desperately to laugh and love again. There were others I was praying for as well, including my husband, son, and daughter. I made it through the fast by the grace of God.

Other Forms of Treatment

I had begun to break through my problems, and the light seemed to stay on longer in my dark closet. I did find that I needed to talk to someone who understood what I was going through, because there were days that I felt well and other days that I felt really down. I never doubted the power of God in my life and I pray I never will, but he put people on this earth for a reason, so I used the resources available to me. On different occasions, I had tried to talk to some family members about my feelings about myself and my daughter, but no one seem to really connect with what I felt.

During this time, I was still working on nursing school and had also decided to get another degree. I decided to take a public health course in maternal and child health. It was there that I learned not to feel guilty about my shortcomings as a mother. My professor taught the different aspects of being a mother and was honest with the class about her own experiences. *Now, I thought to myself, if her children have no special needs, (though she might argue that point) and she is finding difficulty at times with parenting, I have no reason to feel bad. I just need to correct the things that can be improved, apologize for what I have done wrong, and not feel like the world is over when I am not at the top of the mountain all of the time.* In this class, we also discussed the constant judgment that goes on amongst mothers. Mothers can be very critical of each other because sometimes somewhere in their own lives they feel inadequate. It also may make some of them feel better, knowing that someone else is doing a worse job than they are in the mommy-hood department. It would be nice if we could encourage each other with the hope that it would decrease some of the tension we feel when we are out shopping or doing other things while our children begin to act as if they have no home training. Why do we judge each other so? Is it not better to be kind and loving to one another with the understanding that all of us fall short of perfection? I have been in that position of seeing a child fall on the floor and throw a tantrum while the mom seems to have no control. All eyes are on her as she either ignores the child or grabs him harshly and picks him up while yelling. I remember thinking once, *That boy just needs some good discipline and to be told no.* But that was until my daughter did it to me and I could not spank her because at the time she was a foster child. Spanking probably was not the best solution for her anyway because of her history of abuse, yet there I was feeling abusive, panicked, and out of control. I could feel eyes on me as I told her no and then she began to grab everything on the shelf. I literally wanted to smack her, dump her, and run. Does that sound Christian-like? No, it sure does not, but it was true, and the truth will set you free. Going to the grocery store with her was stressful, so I learned to minimize the amount of time we spent in the store together. Once in awhile, my mom would watch her when I went to the grocery store. Other times I would try to plan to shop just before picking her up from school. This child had been desperate for food in her life and had not received it consistently in her infancy and early toddler years. Food created a great deal of anxiety for her, so the grocery store was not a good place for us to be together in the early part of our relationship. After years of stability and being nurtured, we can now go with minimal problems, though I still avoid it when I can.

Parents with special-needs children experience parenting in a way that many would or could not tolerate. Statistics show that children with special needs have a higher chance of being abused than children who are not. This is not to say that the average child will not experience it, because clearly abuse happens in families from all walks of life and it is simply wrong. However, a decrease in stress for parents and caregivers is vitally important so that these types of things will happen less often.

As I mentioned before, you need to know your limitations. Sometimes your heart wants to do what your body and mind cannot handle. Realize that what you give is a lot, and learn to make the time for yourself even if it feels impossible. Do not depend on others to understand you, because many will not, and do not be upset when they don't. Accept help when you can get it, and don't feel bad when the babysitter or the family member comes back with your child(ren) and says, "They were so good with me" as if to say, "I don't know what you are doing wrong, but I did it right." Guess what! After a certain age, how many children do you know who act better with their parents than they do with others? There are very few, if any. Children often feel close and most comfortable with their parents, so they often act out with their parents more. It is with you that they will test for love and security. And with foster children or children with special needs, this occurs more frequently and more intensely. Again, don't take it personally; understand that it will happen and move on. Your value as a parent should not be based on other people's perceptions, ideas, and thoughts. It'll kill you emotionally, and then you will find yourself more frustrated with your children because it seems to be impossible to live up to these standards.

Another thing that I did was reach out for post-adoption support services. It helped me stop playing the blame game and face myself and the ugly truth about being frustrated and angry. I read material that was related to the circumstances. I saw that I was not alone in my feelings and that it was all quite normal when dealing with children with severe traumatic backgrounds. I just kept thinking, *I am not alone and someone gets it* and began to apply some of the principles. I learned that I could gain some control over my daughter's behavior just by changing my methods. Now, what I am going to tell you is going to seem quite simple, but I honestly could not accept doing it before because I was determined not to let her break me. I had been broken too many times before, and I refused to let her think she had control. The weird thing is that she did have control. Every time she provoked me to react to her behavior, I reacted negatively. When she yelled, I'd yell louder. When she threw a tantrum, I'd get angry. When she called me so many times I thought I would go insane, I'd tell her to leave me alone or go to her room. She had been so used to reactions that included yelling, anger, and rejection that she was trying to get me to give her what she knew as "the norm." It sounds a little odd, but it was so true. Most children do not get to choose what family they are born into or who will adopt them, but they learn very early on how to get certain reactions. The new way was to not react negatively to her screaming but to say to her, "What is getting you so upset that you feel like you have to scream?" Or when she would have a tantrum, I'd say, "You must really be upset to act that way, because I know when you are feeling good, you are a much nicer person." When I first read some examples of how to change my reactions, I thought it was a bit ridiculous and a bit too much. Now, for a child who is nonverbal, behavior modification can be even more challenging. Fortunately, she was verbal (a little too verbal) and could understand me. When I saw it made things better, I could not stop. I was finding new ways every day to connect with my daughter, and I started to feel more in control as a parent. I felt less disrespected and more appreciated. I had felt for quite some time that she should at least try to be a good child since we had tried so desperately to love her, but I had to change my reactions for her to understand that I was truly different from what she had previously experienced.

The days are better, not perfect. She still has some difficulty focusing, staying on task, and learning. Some of her annoying habits are not broken and are on a much deeper subconscious level, but my goodness, it is possible now to live with her in peace and even enjoy some good moments in between.

I used to worry about her future and how difficult she would be as a young adult. We will cross that bridge when we get to it, and if we cannot cross the bridge with her, we will help guide her so that she can cross it to get the help she needs while knowing all along that she is loved.

I am done blaming myself for every little or even big error. I am done worrying about what everyone else thinks or feels. I am human with flaws. My heart's intentions are good. My mind is much clearer, and my spirit has been changed by God. Now I just have to live regardless of the troubles in life and not try to do too much at one time. You do the same. Live wonderfully—don't just barely survive.

A Better Relationship with God

All of the experiences over the years just led me to be closer to God. I was angry with him for a long time but still loved him and would always return to him. *One of the lessons that I needed to learn was to have a daily relationship with him that was not based on him giving me everything I wanted.* Neither was it based on the maltreatment I received from people but on his love. God's love does not give up, and continues when humans get tired. He was also trying to teach me to love others with his love and not my own. This became apparent when the love that I had once felt for my daughter turned into resentment and bitterness. I did not want her to leave, though I thought about it so many times, I lost count. I also thought of leaving. I no longer had what it took to stay or to love. I prayed for his love to dwell and for his strength to help me get through, and he did just that. Emotionally, I let her go. She no longer weighed down my heart. I stopped trying to control her, because it took too much energy from me. I could not make my family do what I wanted either. Each individual is responsible for his or her own choices. Before I was married or a mom, I was an individual, as are they. Yes, they do things to annoy me, as I am sure I have done to them, but it's not the end of the world when they do. Surely, it is not worth me losing my salvation over it. I refuse to spend eternity without the Lord. When I asked God to help me truly find him, he did just that and not in the way I expected. I felt like he allowed flames upon me, but when I came out, I looked a little more like gold than the tainted silver I had been before. *I am sure there will be more flames to come, but it's better to be in the fire of life with God than to be in chaos with man.* Shortly after I asked God to help me find him, he gave me these words:

Find Me

Find me
and you shall see,
and see me for me,

that I am God of heaven, who knows all things.

I make wrong right and I take away the shame.
Look for me in your dark hours.
Worship me in your bright hours.

Praise me when it's raining
and I'll send you flowers.

Sometimes my people wonder where I am in their difficulty.
They wonder why I don't change things according to their realities.
But I am there.
Still wondering where I am?
Call me and I will answer.

Stop trusting in folks and their ways.
Just because you don't see, that
doesn't mean that I am not still the same,
yesterday, today, and forevermore.

Some of you wonder why others seem to get away with sinning
and never seem to suffer from it.
But they do
in their spirits when there is no rest,
when they are crying inside in so much distress.

And still I say that you need to look to me for the solutions.
Look for me in your quiet moments.

Calm your mind, so you can hear
I am near.

No, I am not going to strike them down
with the might of my hand
and pay them back
according to your plan.

"Vengeance is mine," says the Lord.
I will repay.
If I paid everybody back according to the people that they hurt,
there would not be many
people left on the earth.

People are broken in places sometimes
that the naked eye cannot see.

And yet you judge them according to their deeds.

I see the heart and their potential.
I see the end and not the middle.

Sometimes I have to let the mess be known
before I can heal the brokenness of their moan,
the groaning of the soul,
the one that is so deep that sometimes they don't even know.

Getting tired of me telling you to love those that despitefully use you?
Tired of forgiving your brother and sister 70x7?
How many times have I forgiven you?
Time after time,
even for your evil thoughts and actions.

And even as I reveal these things to you,
it is not to condemn you,
but for you to remember that you are all sinners saved by grace.
So put down the mace, the spiritual mace,
the one you walk around with
to prevent yourself from being harmed,
the cold shoulder you give so that so-and-so will know
that you are simply just not in the mood for their mess today.

Broken dreams and held-in tears
can lead to anger
that can take the paint off the car
because you become like acid,
burning holes in things that never saw you coming.
Be careful to look to me
and find me in your difficult moments
so that you will not be found in secret doing things
that I am saddened by.

No, you are not perfect,
but you can have a perfect heart toward me.
Seek me, find me,
and I shall answer you in your pain.

I hear you when you call,
but do you hear me when I answer?

Or do you begin to say
that I don't love you?

How can you think that I don't love my children?
Love does not mean that everything will go your way
or that you will never be corrected in your wrong.
It means that no matter what, to the ends of the earth,
I will love you.

And because I want you to dwell in my presence for eternity,
I will correct you.
I will warn you of what is to come.
I will also, though, hug you and rest upon your head
as you lie in bed.

I will sing to you through the night
and send my angels so that you can be led
to the right places and the right things.

Seek me.
Find me and I will be there,
simply because I love you,
simply because I care for you,
simply because you belong to me.

My Plans Change

Since I was eighteen years of age, I had been in the medical field in some shape or form. I worked as a nurse's aide, medical assistant, and dialysis technician, and had decided to go to school to get a bachelor's degree in nursing. During that time I had chosen a minor in sociology. I realized that I did very well in it and soon began to lean toward the idea of social services. However, I had completed all of my prerequisites for nursing, so I began to apply to different schools to complete my clinical rotations. It just did not seem to work out, and I graduated with a bachelor's degree in another field, hoping to use it one day for a bridge program to become an APRN (advanced practice registered nurse). In addition, I later had an injury to my back, neck, and right hip from an automobile accident that prevented me from standing for long periods of time. A truck hit me, flipping my car. I was trapped in the car for what seemed like forever. Every window was shattered. It is amazing that a main artery was not severed. I was out of work for three months. I was not a spring chicken that could recover quickly from injuries anymore. So unless a miracle happened, I could not return to school for nursing.

Before the accident, somewhere in the process of dealing with issues that surrounded my daughter, I had prayed and asked God to not let everything that I had experienced be for nothing, and he did just that. Soon afterward, I began to work in social services helping children and their families, particularly in the areas of parenting, disciplining techniques, parenting advocacy, and counseling. These services help to prevent children from being removed from their homes. I would have not imagined that I would go from being a nursing major to doing social work, but God knew. It has been quite an experience and I plan to further my education as time allows, but I have learned the most by listening to the quiet whispers of the Lord that bring about change and peace. There is a verse in the Bible that reads, "What shall we say then? Shall we continue in sin that grace may abound? God forbid" (Romans 6:1–2 KJV). We often make excuses for ourselves by blaming others but not looking at our inner selves. It is often true that there are those around us who do things they should not, but we cannot make them change. And why do we not question more, "What can I do to change?" Often when we began to change, things can seem clearer and we make better choices. It may even seem that those who appeared to be so irritating before become less irritating. Their behaviors may be the same, but you have chosen not to react in a negative manner to them. And wonderfully, once the garbage has been cleaned out of you, you may be able to find more compassion for others. There will be those that you will find may have to leave your life because they are toxic to your emotional healing, but cut the others a little slack and live a little more calmly. It may very well be your road to peace. That road to peace is not based on everything going perfectly in your life. It's inner peace that resides even when everything around you is in chaos. "And the peace of God, which passeth all understanding, shall keep your hearts and minds through Christ Jesus" (Philippians 4:7 KJV).

Never Quite Comfortable
but Wise

I have learned not to ever get too comfortable with Mary. She has a way of keeping me on my toes. We have even had The Department of Children and Families show up at our house to question us. Thankfully, the social worker saw that we were good parents and that Mary was well taken care of and dropped the investigation. Months later, Mary stole $180.00 from my husband's wallet and lied about it for an entire week, until the babysitter told us she had it in her book bag. The disturbing thing is that she asked for lunch money every school morning, as if she did not have any. She lied without batting an eye. And after she was found out, she still tried to lie. The first lie: A guy was riding on a bike and dropped it and I picked it up. The second lie: My friend gave it to me. The third lie: I found it in the lunchroom—the lunch lady gave it to me. My husband finally yelled, "Tell the truth." My husband rarely yells. She looked up and said, "Okay, Ill tell the truth," and she did. We were deeply hurt by her actions. No one in our home needs to steal. We are very giving. But it was not the first time, and it probably will not be the last.

At times I had been warned by the quickening of the holy-spirit. "But if the spirit of him that raised up Jesus from the dead dwell in you, he that raised up Christ from the dead shall also quicken your mortal bodies by his spirit that dwelleth in you" (Romans 8:11

KJV). The times that I had heeded warnings I was wise but when I did not listen, I have paid dearly.

It is hard to explain the spirit of the Lord and how it will warn you if you don't have it, so please receive it so you can understand. It simply starts by asking for forgiveness of your sins and humbling yourself to the God of heaven. It is also important to understand that Jesus died for you to give you life. The shedding of his blood on the cross is what makes it possible for you to receive his spirit. Let him in and he will transform your life and give you a clean heart that wants to please him. He will also give you a new language, one that you will know without a doubt has come from heaven. The Holy Spirit is a guide if you let it be. It is a corrector if you listen, and a protector in the time of trouble. Don't be afraid. It is also wise enough to be gentle. Gentleness is one of the fruits of the spirit.

I wish that day I had spoken less and followed the lead, but you live and you learn. "Wherefore, my beloved brethren, let every man be swift to hear, slow to speak, slow to wrath" (James 1:19 KJV).

We made it through that unfortunate situation, and I took it as an opportunity to parent a little more gently. With this came peace. Though dealing with difficult behaviors can be unnerving, being a foster or adoptive parent is bigger than you or me. It's about kingdom building. All souls belong to God, and I am sure that God does not want his little children walking around wounded with no soft place to fall. We should be one of those soft places. They already know what harshness is like. It is not an easy calling to care for the orphaned, but it is a necessary one nonetheless. "You shall not afflict any widow or fatherless child" (Exodus 22:22 KJV).

I also prayed against spiritual forces that try to destroy what

God puts together. In addition to that I prayed against the spirits of abuse that control people's lives and torture them. "For we wrestle not against flesh and blood but against principalities, against powers, against the rulers of the darkness of this world, against spiritual wickedness in high places" (Ephesians 6:12 KJV). Some might not think that prayer is necessary, but I know that it is. Prayer changes things. Also, understand that the devil does not care if you are a child or an adult. He will come after anyone he thinks may effectively make a difference to the kingdom of God. I believe this is why so many of us have been abused and misused as children. If he can break us, then God can't make us into what he desires for us to be. God will not push past our will or take away our freedom to choose. Childhood trauma if not healed will negatively affect adulthood and strip from an individual their joy, peace, and love. Often people cannot comprehend why they were hurt as a child because children have a certain innocence that should be protected but often is not. I ask you from my heart not to let this stop you from living free and walking into the calling of your life. And though the sin of the abuser may seem great, the Bible reminds us that "all have sinned and come short of the glory of God" (Romans 3:23 KJV).

The Miracle

Just writing this chapter makes me smile, because this book has been in progress for years. Before the accident, I had finally started to feel normal again. My physical energy had returned. I was starting to have moments of joy. After the accident, I started to feel depressed again. I was able to be intimate with my husband on only one occasion while I was out of work because I was in pain. This information under normal circumstances would not be anyone else's business, but I share it with you because it is how our little miracle was conceived. After all the many years we had been together, life came forth from that one time. I could have been dead, but our Lord chose to give me life at one of my weakest moments. It reminded me of another Scripture: "For the sake of Christ, then I am content with weaknesses, insults, hardships, persecutions and calamities. For when I am weak, then I am strong" (2 Corinthians 12:10 KJV). With pain and discomfort, I made it through, and we welcomed a beautiful baby girl we can call our own. Years ago, in the early chapters, I had called it by faith: "If God sees fit, he will bring forth another child from this womb." "Now faith is the substance of things hoped for, the evidence of things not seen" (Hebrews 11:1 KJV). She is full of joy like I have never seen before. My heart is glad. Our hearts are glad. We are blessed beyond measure.

Hurt Made Well

Over the years, Mary has gone from being in special education and having severe behavioral problems to being a child of example on the honor roll. This is quite an accomplishment for a child whose sanity was in question. The praise belongs to Jesus, because alone I could not help her to the extent that she needed. I would have given in or lost my mind. God gave me strength and continues to equip me for times that are difficult. I had to surrender control to him. I had to bow to the king. My nature is self-driven and very determined, and this unbelievably challenging situation put me on my knees in a way I had never been. I was used to "making things happen," and God reminded me that he "makes things happen" a great deal better than I do. Sometimes it is hard to submit because God's ways are not our own. It appears at times that he does not know what he is doing, but he always does. Don't doubt it for a second! God is alive and real. I will not pretend to always understand his ways, and quite frankly he is not obligated to tell me why he lets things happen that seem cruel. I am learning to trust him. I hope you can too. No one will love you more.

It was hurt that caused me to hate. It was hurt that caused my husband to try drugs. It was hurt that caused my oldest daughter to act out, but we believe that it will not destroy our futures because of our trust in God. Does that mean that everything will go our way? No, but it does mean that we will be okay, because even in death there is life, so what do we have to fear? Nothing!

Over the years, I have learned to love unconditionally and without reservation. I love my family, friends, and foes. All thanks be to God. Again, God is simply amazing!

And our oldest daughter is our little angel who was broken by abuse and is being mended by God's love.